AN
ACRE
OF
TIME
THE
PLAY

An Acre of Time

by
Jason Sherman

inspired by the book of the same title
by Phil Jenkins

Playwrights Canada Press
Toronto • Canada

An Acre of Time: The Play © Copyright 2001 Jason Sherman
inspired by the book of the same title by Phil Jenkins

Playwrights Canada Press
54 Wolseley Street, 2nd Floor
Toronto, Ontario CANADA M5T 1A5
416-703-0201   fax 416-703-0059
info@puc.ca   http://www.puc.ca

Playwrights Canada Press acknowledges the support of The Canada Council for the Arts for our publishing programme and the Ontario Arts Council.

ONTARIO ARTS COUNCIL
CONSEIL DES ARTS DE L'ONTARIO

Cover photo of Susan Coyne by Cylla Von Tiedemann.
Production Manager: Jodi Armstrong

National Library of Canada Cataloguing in Publication Data

Sherman, Jason, 1962-
   An acre of time : inspired by the book of the same name by Phil Jenkins

ISBN 0-88754-609-9

1. Jenkins, Phil, 1951- . Acre of time. I. Jenkins, Phil, 1951- . Acre of time. II. Title.

PS8587.H3858A75 2001   C812'.54   C2001-900738-8
PR9199.3.S5119A75 2001

First edition: July 2001.
Printed and bound by AGMV Marquis at Quebec, Canada.

Dedication:
For my father.

Acknowledgments

Thanks to the many actors who participated in the many workshops of *An Acre of Time*, and in particular to the cast of the premiere production in Ottawa, where it was a very different play: Pierre Brault, Dennis Fitzgerald, Marie-Josée Lefebvre, Catriona Leger, Gordon White and Beverley Wolfe. And special thanks to Phil Jenkins, for the book.

An Acre of Time was first produced at the Tarragon Theatre, Toronto, on March 13, 2001, with the following cast:

Julia Wright	Susan Coyne
Stan & others	David Jansen
Davidson & others	Pierre Brault
Robyn & others	Lisa Norton
Danielle & others	Kristen van Ginhoven
Tom & others	Timothy Hill

Directed by Brian Quirt
Lighting designed by Paul Mathiesen
Set & costume design by Carolyn M. Smith
Music by Ian Tamblyn
Stage managed by Fiona Jones

An earlier version of *An Acre of Time* was produced at the Great Canadian Theatre Company in Ottawa, May 2000.

CHARACTERS

Julia Wright
Stan & others
Davidson & others
Robyn & others
Danielle & others
Tom & others

PRODUCTION NOTE

Character doubling: the First Commissioner also plays Stan, Stegmann, Peter, LeBreton and Jankov; the Second, Robyn, Louise, LeBreton's nieces and Rebekah; the Third, Tom; the Fourth, Davidson, Bill, Champlain, Dalhousie, Auguste, Louis, and an Irishman; the Fifth, Danielle, a waitress, Madame de Champlain, and Dolores.

ACT ONE

THE COMMISSION

JULIA Wright, a surveyor, appears before five members of a commission.

FIRST COMMISSIONER   You were asked to survey the LeBreton Flats and report your findings.

SECOND COMMISSIONER   The LeBreton Flats currently sit empty. A field covered in weeds.

THIRD COMMISSIONER   The Commission wishes to redevelop the Flats. Among the plans are: mixed-income housing, parkland, government buildings, access to the river, an eternal flame.

FOURTH COMMISSIONER   The report you have filed is most unusual. It contains opinions.

FIFTH COMMISSIONER   You write of "rituals." Of "respect." Of "rebirth."

FIRST COMMISSIONER   You write of "natural states," yet you do not acknowledge that the most natural state for the Flats is the purpose to which the state chooses to put it.

FIFTH COMMISSIONER   You sent this report to the Minister, who has demanded an explanation.

FIRST COMMISSIONER   As do we.

JULIA   I was approached a month ago by my superior in the Department of Surveys.

STAN'S OFFICE

STAN	Morning, Julia.
JULIA	Morning, Stan.
STAN	Is that a new outfit?
JULIA	I don't think so.
STAN	Well, I've never noticed it before. It's very becoming.

Pause.

JULIA	You wanted to see me?
STAN	Yes. I have a job for you. By the river, near the Parliament Buildings. Not that you'd know there's a river there, what with the parkway and all. Come, you can see it from here.

Leads her to the window.

LeBreton Flats. Know it?

Pause.

Julia?

JULIA	I've been there once or twice.
SECOND COMMISSIONER	*And had you?*
JULIA	*I'll come to that.*

STAN shows her a map.

STAN	Well, if the Commission has its way, you'll be going a lot more than that. We all will. Here we are. Nice little square. 160 acres waiting to be brought back to life. Is that a new perfume?

JULIA	I don't know. I don't wear perfume.
STAN	Ah. Must be my cologne. (*beat*) The Commission's owned most of this area for some time. The fields, the shoreline... it's the streets... that have always eluded us.
JULIA	Stan?
STAN	Hm?
JULIA	The streets.
STAN	Yes. Owned by the city. Until last week. Now they're ours. So we need a survey.
JULIA	Look, I'm up to my eyeballs. Couldn't you send–
STAN	Believe me, I wouldn't bother you with this if I didn't have to. Bit of a rush on it, I'm afraid. The Planning Department's done up the concept map. You just need to make sure the streets that are here match up with the ones down there. (*handing over the map*) I've marked out a starting point for you.
JULIA	Very thoughtful.
STAN	Yes, well. (*beat*) Take Danielle with you. Oh, and, what's her name, the summer student.
JULIA	Look, this is going to be hard enough without having to show some board member's daughter "the ropes."
STAN	Alright, alright. Just do me this one favour, would you? If she proves to be any trouble, any trouble at all, I'll reassign her. Deal?
JULIA	Fine. Anything else?
STAN	Well. Are you busy this weekend?

JULIA	Yes.
STAN	Even for a coffee?
JULIA	It's not you.
STAN	It's me asking. Perhaps you have someone.

Pause.

STAN Tell you what. In case you change your mind, I'll give you my home number. (*looking for a pencil*) Damn, can't find a pencil. That's the trouble with all these computers, there's no need for pencils anymore. I put in a request for supplies two weeks ago. All I want is a pencil – a simple stupid–. Let me know if you need anything.

JULIA (*to the commission*) I handed out the research assignments. I went to Central Surveys, sent Danielle to the records office and the student—Robyn—to the archives. We began our field work the following week, and were joined by Davidson, from Planning and Design.

THE FLATS

JULIA looks through the surveying equipment at DANIELLE, holding the rod. ROBYN stands near JULIA, observing. DAVIDSON is drawing sketches.

DANIELLE 49-26-57. (*beat*) 73-20-21.

DAVIDSON Hut-hut-hut.

ROBYN What are those numbers?

DAVIDSON does a bird whistle: two short sharp notes.

DANIELLE	Degrees, minutes, seconds.
	DAVIDSON: bird whistle.
DAVIDSON	(*to ROBYN*) Hot, isn't it?
ROBYN	(*to JULIA*) What do you see through there?
JULIA	Mm?
ROBYN	What do you see?
JULIA	A rod. Danielle, move left.
	DAVIDSON does another bird whistle.
ROBYN	Can I try?
JULIA	"Try"?
ROBYN	Can I have a look?
JULIA	Look, sweetheart. This isn't a toy.
ROBYN	I know that. It's a very powerful instrument.
JULIA	Yeah. And it costs a lot of money. And time is money, and we're short on both.
	DAVIDSON: bird whistle.
	Davidson.
ROBYN	Can you tell me how it works, then?
JULIA	How what works?
ROBYN	The – whatever it's called.
JULIA	It's not in your line.
ROBYN	Does it measure acres?

JULIA	No, it – look–

DAVIDSON: bird whistle.

Davidson!

DAVIDSON	What?
JULIA	Do you mind?
DAVIDSON	'Scuse me for breathing.
JULIA	Breathe. Just don't whistle.

JULIA continues her work. ROBYN starts measuring out paces.

DAVIDSON	Supposed to hit 40 today. That's not good. Hard to breathe when it hits 40.
ROBYN	Miss Wright, did you know the Germans used a branch to measure out acres? Just an ordinary branch, 16 feet long.
JULIA	Marvellous.
ROBYN	I did some extra research. I mean, I know how you said I should just "stick to the facts," but I got to thinking, like, wouldn't it be amazing to know what was here before? I got so much stuff. I went to the National Archives, they have tons of stuff. Like, there used to be a forest here. There were so many trees you'd have to squeeze between the trunks just to–
JULIA	Okay, let's – let's *skip* the history lesson. Okay?

DAVIDSON: bird whistle.

Danielle, move left.

DANIELLE	You get that last point?

JULIA	I said move, so I guess that means I got the point.
DANIELLE	Well I didn't see you write it down.
JULIA	Okay, I'm writing it down. Can we do this? Before we all melt?
DAVIDSON	So, kid, how'd they do that? The Germans, I mean. With the branch.
ROBYN	Well. They'd mark a spot with a stone. Then turn the branch end to end, forty times; the first side. Mark it with a stone. Then four turns for the second side. Another marker. Then forty–

As she walks along, she turns into LOUISE, JULIA's daughter.

LOUISE	Oh mummy look! Chicory. And clover. And here. White daisies! He loves me, he loves me not, he loves me, he loves me not...
FIRST COMMISSIONER	*Why tell us about your daughter?*
JULIA	*I had been here with her. A picnic. The student reminded me of her.*
FOURTH COMMISSIONER	*Continue.*
ROBYN	And voila, an acre.

DAVIDSON: bird whistle.

DAVIDSON	How 'bout that.
DANIELLE	Julia?
JULIA	Yeah.
DANIELLE	Everything alright?

JULIA	Yeah. The heat's playing tricks with the instruments.
FIRST COMMISSIONER	*Was that true?*
JULIA	*Of course not.*
DAVIDSON	(*to ROBYN*) You find that out at the archives, eh?
ROBYN	Mm hm. I found out tons of stuff.
DAVIDSON	When did you do all this?
ROBYN	On the weekend.
DAVIDSON	Weekend, eh? That's how you spend your weekends?
ROBYN	I don't mind.
DAVIDSON	Don't you have a boyfriend?
DANIELLE	I win!
JULIA	Right.
	JULIA hands DANIELLE ten bucks.
DAVIDSON	What's that about?
DANIELLE	We had a bet about how long it would take you to ask her if she has a boyfriend.
DAVIDSON	Oh, that's funny.
DANIELLE	Julia thought you'd do it by asking if she'd like to see your sketches.
DAVIDSON	Hey. I'm just making conversation. Know what I mean? *Conversation.*

JULIA	(*to the commission*) Our work continued. By mid-morning, the heat was unbearable. And so was Davidson.
	DAVIDSON: bird whistle.
	Davidson, how many times must I ask you to stop whistling?
DAVIDSON	Okay. Let me point something out here. (*He points to JULIA and DANIELLE.*) Department of Surveys. (*He points to himself.*) Department of Planning and Design. Don't tell me what to do.
DANIELLE	Asshole.
DAVIDSON	Just supremely confident.
	DAVIDSON starts to take off his shirt.
DANIELLE	Must you?
DAVIDSON	Drives you crazy, doesn't it?
DANIELLE	You're pathetic, Davidson.
JULIA	Davidson, put your shirt on.
DAVIDSON	Once again, allow me to point out that–
JULIA	Davidson, put your goddamned shirt on. You're *hot*, okay, fine. So are we. Look, do you need to be *right here?* I mean, can't you do your drawings *over there?* Is there some particular advantage to your standing right here?
DANIELLE	Maybe we should take a break, hm?
JULIA	Fine.
	They break.

FIRST COMMISSIONER	*Miss Wright, these details — how are they relevant to your findings?*
JULIA	*You have asked me to defend an unusual report. You must allow me to do so in an unusual way.*
THIRD COMMISSIONER	*Continue.*
ROBYN	Listen. Do you hear it?
	They listen.
DAVIDSON	I hear cars.
ROBYN	No. The falls. When Samuel de Champlain came up the Ottawa River, looking for the passage to China?
DAVIDSON	This more of your "research?"
ROBYN	Mm hm. He wrote in his notebook that you could hear the falls for two leagues. It's June 13, 1613. Champlain is 46 years old. He has a 13-year-old wife back home in France.
DAVIDSON	What the hell's he doing over here, then?
ROBYN	Looking for the spice route. With his Indian guides, from the Kichesippirini tribe, he paddles up the Ottawa river, right over there. He makes note of the islands, and the falls. "This waterfall makes such a noise in this basin that it can be heard for more than two leagues away." Then the guides explain the ceremony of throwing tobacco into the falls, to calm the angry water spirits.
DAVIDSON	For what?

ROBYN

For the lives that were taken by the river. Must have freaked out Champlain. He couldn't swim.

> *JULIA walks away as ROBYN continues.*

When the Kichesippirini lived here, they thought of themselves as part of nature. Spirits of the gods were everywhere. In rocks, trees, the earth. They lived here, they hunted here, they dreamed here, and when they died, they were reborn here. Isn't it wonderful to think that way?

> *Pause. ROBYN becomes LOUISE, picking flowers, as JULIA recalls the picnic.*

LOUISE

Know what these are, Daddy?

BILL

Daisies.

LOUISE

Precisely. And these?

BILL

Mm...

LOUISE

Viper's bugloss.

BILL

Bugloss?

LOUISE

Bu-gloss! They used to use it to cure snakebites.

BILL

How do you know this? How does she know this?

LOUISE

Cause I'm so smart.

BILL

You are. (*sings*) "I wish I was in Carrickfergus/If only for nights in Ballygrand."

LOUISE

Oh no, my bracelet! My bracelet fell off. It must be here somewhere. Mummy, can you help me?

DANIELLE	Julia?
JULIA	Yeah.
DANIELLE	We should get started.
JULIA	Right. (*looks around*) Where's Robyn?
DANIELLE	She went to look at the falls.
DAVIDSON	What's left of 'em.
DANIELLE	You okay?
JULIA	Fine.
DANIELLE	Maybe we should knock off for the day. This sun...
JULIA	Let's just get this done. (*to the commission*) And we got back to our work. A half hour passed, and Robyn did not return. I sent Danielle to find her while I continued the survey on my own.
DAVIDSON	Forget about the kid. She's fine. You guys really have a bet?
JULIA	Yup.
DAVIDSON	That's low.
JULIA	Suffer.
DAVIDSON	I mean, I was just making conversation.
JULIA	She's 17.
DAVIDSON	She is very mature. And I'm not talking about her in a physical kind of way.
JULIA	No no.

DAVIDSON	I'm talking mental-wise. 'Cause not all girls develop at the same rate. And I'll tell you something else. When she was talking about Champlain, and his 13 year-old-wife? She was looking right at me.
JULIA	Is that right?
DAVIDSON	I swear!
JULIA	You were born in the wrong century, Davidson.
DAVIDSON	Don't I know it! Still, you think it was a sign?
JULIA	Yeah. "Watch for children."
	Enter TOM.
TOM	Afternoon, gentlefolk.
DAVIDSON	How you doing?
TOM	Keeping cool.
DAVIDSON	Yeah? How you managing that?
TOM	(*nodding in the direction of his trailer*) AC in the trailer.
DAVIDSON	Right on. What's with the snaps?
TOM	Oh. I'm a scout.
DAVIDSON	Scout? Like– (*does Hollywood Indian war cry*) –like that?
TOM	Yeah. Just like that.
DAVIDSON	You know, it's funny. Just above your head right now, I see a cartoon bubble. It says, "what an asshole." Seriously, though, what, scout, what.

TOM	Location scout. For a film.
DAVIDSON	A film. Alright. What's it about?
TOM	Land claims.
DAVIDSON	Land – you know, there has not been a decent land claims movie since, uh, since, what, since forever really. Breaking new ground there, my friend. Me, I'm kind of an action film buff myself.
TOM	Oh, there's action.
DAVIDSON	Like what, a canoe chase? (*rowing an imaginary oar*) "Hurry, Little Bear, white man has speed boat." Oops, there goes that bubble again.
JULIA	You'll have to excuse Davidson. God knows we try to.
TOM	I didn't get your name.
JULIA	Julia.
TOM	Tom. What's your story?
JULIA	Survey for the National Capital Commission.
TOM	Oh yeah. Eternal flame, huh?
DAVIDSON	That's part of it yeah. But there's a lot more to it than...
	TOM's paying him no attention. He's staring at JULIA.
JULIA	Is there something I can do for you?
TOM	Yeah. Smile. (*He snaps her picture.*) I needed a shot of the background.

DAVIDSON	Uh huh. Listen, if you don't mind, we've got some work to do.
JULIA	(*to the commission*) It was then we heard the sound of a partridge.
TOM	Constant Penency.
JULIA	What?
TOM	The partridge. That's Constant Penency.

ROBYN and DANIELLE come back.

DANIELLE	Hey! I found her!
JULIA	What happened? Where have you been?
ROBYN	I–I–
JULIA	What is it?
ROBYN	I saw him.
JULIA	Who?
ROBYN	Champlain... I was standing on the shore... I looked down and I saw him, paddling along the river... there was a girl with him... they looked up at me, called to me to join them...
DAVIDSON	Heat stroke.
DANIELLE	Let's get her some shade.
DAVIDSON	There is no shade.
TOM	We can take her to my trailer. Come on.
DAVIDSON	I got her. I got her. Easy does it. Come on – come on–

They lead her off.

JULIA	(*to the commission*) Robyn was fine, but by then the heat had made it impossible to carry on with our work. I packed up and began to walk home. Dark clouds began to form. I stopped into a restaurant to wait out the approaching storm.

THE RESTAURANT

JULIA sits at a table. WAITRESS approaches.

WAITRESS	Are you alone?
JULIA	Very.
WAITRESS	A drink to start?
JULIA	No. Yes. Wine.
WAITRESS	By the glass, we have–
JULIA	A bottle.
WAITRESS	We have a lovely merlot.
JULIA	Fine. What are your specials?
WAITRESS	Do you like birds?
JULIA	I'm game.
WAITRESS	We have a succulent squab.
JULIA	Never heard of it.
WAITRESS	Pigeon. It was very popular in the 1800s. It's making a comeback.
JULIA	Not tonight, it isn't. What else?
WAITRESS	How do you feel about partridge?

JULIA	(*beat*) How's it served?
WAITRESS	On a piece of toast. It's a little crunchy.
JULIA	The toast?
WAITRESS	The bird.
JULIA	Right. I'll give it a shot.

> *The WAITRESS goes. STAN, holding a drink, approaches her.*

STAN	I don't believe it.
JULIA	Me neither.
STAN	This is my neighborhood restaurant. I eat in here practically every night! Mind? (*off her hesitation*) At least have a drink with me.
JULIA	Sure.

> *The WAITRESS brings the wine, then goes.*

STAN	How'd it go today?
JULIA	Oh, terrific.
STAN	Good, good. How's Robyn working out, then, eh?
JULIA	Very – she's fine.
STAN	Good, good. She's something, I'll tell you. All that "research." She doesn't understand: the Commission is *not* interested in history.

> *Pause.*

So, nothing unusual to report?

JULIA	Well, it was hot.
STAN	Oh, my, yes.
JULIA	The level was bubbling up, made it difficult to go on.
STAN	Oh, you don't have to explain.
JULIA	You asked.
STAN	(*beat*) Sometimes I miss being in the field. Yes, yes. Stuck in that office. Dealing with the politics of it, and all that. Nasty business.
JULIA	We're well out of it.
STAN	Oh yes. Not our concern, really. No. Finding out where the lines are, that's our concern.
JULIA	Indeed.
	Pause.
STAN	Everything alright then?
JULIA	Look, Stan–
STAN	Please, I – Julia, I don't pretend to know you very well. Of course that's not from lack of trying. It's just that I find myself wanting to know if, well this will sound old-fashioned, but to know if you're happy. Because that's a thing to strive for, isn't it? To be happy?
JULIA	I'm not so sure.
STAN	You're not?
JULIA	I'm not so sure it's something you can try to be, or something you can only remember being.

STAN   Oh. I hadn't expected you to say that. (*beat*)
              This is a difficult time for me. Next week,
              it's the third anniversary of my wife's
              death. No, please. After I lost her, I, I didn't
              think I wanted to go on. They say it's easier
              for men, but, damn it, for me, it – well, she
              was the only woman I'd ever been with.
              Can you believe that? I'm forty years old,
              and in all that time – one woman. That's
              something, eh?

JULIA   It really is, Stan.

STAN   Yes. She was all I ever wanted. I never so
              much as looked at another woman in all
              that time. Oh alright, I looked, what's a
              man supposed to do? Damn it, it's the
              drink. I swear it's the drink. Well. Last
              night, the damndest thing happened. I was
              getting into bed. I don't sleep well and all
              that, and sometimes I have a hard time
              distinguishing between something in a
              dream and something in the real world.
              But this was different, you see. I was lying
              there, when I heard it. A voice, her voice,
              whispering in my ear. "Let me go," she
              said. Yes, yes, I'm sure of it. "Let me go."
              And I realized, my god, I realized right
              then that I *hadn't* let her go. I was selfishly
              holding onto her. She couldn't go on, her
              spirit, I mean, and I couldn't go on.
              Couldn't let myself think that I might ever
              be happy again. Why do we do that? Hold
              on to our tragedies? This morning, I took
              her ring—it was the first thing of hers I
              saw—I took it and I flung it into the river,
              and with that act, Julia, I, I suddenly felt a
              release, a great release. Do you know what
              I'm saying?

              BILL appears.

BILL   I don't know what happened. We were in
              the canoe. A perfect day. The wind picked
              up. It started to rain, to pour. The canoe

tipped over. I grabbed her hand, she
slipped away. I grabbed it again, something
pulled at her, pulled, pulled her down. I
tried. I did. I tried. I couldn't, Julia – Julia–

STAN   Tell you what. Change the subject.
              Have I ever shown you my architectural
              drawings? Surprised, aren't you? Yes. I was
              going to be an architect. That was the plan.
              Well. The workload was something. 80
              hour weeks. And so competitive!

BILL   I don't know what happened.

STAN   I'm just not that sort of animal. Anyway,
              I'm in a related field.

BILL   I grabbed her hand, she slipped away.

STAN   I'm well paid. And I'm still a young man,
              so I can always get back to it. And other
              lies.

BILL   Something pulled at her.

STAN   Anyway, I'd love to know what you make
              of them, my drawings. Your opinion means
              a lot to me.

BILL   Julia...

STAN   Now don't misconstrue this for... I thought
              you could come out to the house... perhaps
              this weekend, or next... and...

BILL   Julia...

JULIA   (to STAN) Christ! Leave me alone, would
              you? If you want me to "be happy"?
              Alright?

STAN   Of course. If that's what... of course.

              He goes. The WAITRESS brings the bird.

JULIA	What is this?
WAITRESS	The partridge.
JULIA	The head's still on.
WAITRESS	Of course.
JULIA	The *head* is–
WAITRESS	Would you like something else?
JULIA	No.
WAITRESS	I can order–
JULIA	I don't want anything else. Just take it away.

The WAITRESS takes the plate and goes.

(*to the commission*) I finished the wine. I started to walk again. The wind began to pick up. I found myself at the Flats. On the spot where we'd been that morning, where Robyn had measured out an acre. I thought about her, how like my daughter she was, and how unlike her. Through the howling wind, I could hear, faintly, the sound of the falls, the water rushing past to reach the ocean.

LOUISE and BILL appear.

LOUISE	Mother, please!
BILL	Come on, Julia, I've been away a lot this year. You said the two of us should spend more time together, so I–
LOUISE	We're going to take the train, and rent a cottage, and go sailing, oh mother, please, please, please, please.

BILL	Forget it, kid.
LOUISE	Oh!
BILL	No, no. Your mother's tacit disapproval has reared it's–
JULIA	You could at least have–
BILL	You can't control her every move.
LOUISE	Please don't fight. Please! We're having such a lovely day. Mother. It's just for the weekend. It'll be so much fun. Please let me go. Please let me go! I'll never never never ask again, I promise!
BILL	I need time with her too, Julia.
LOUISE	Look.

> *BILL does a bird whistle.*

	It's a partridge.
BILL	See that? It's a sign.

> *DANIELLE jumps out at her, shining a flashlight.*

DANIELLE	Hee-ya!
JULIA	Jesus Christ!
DANIELLE	Ha ha ha!
JULIA	Oh Christ – Danielle!
DANIELLE	Sorry – ha ha ha! I couldn't resist! Ha ha ha! I saw you coming!
JULIA	What are you *doing?*

DANIELLE Looking for my papers. In all the excitement with the kid, I forgot to pack them.

JULIA You find them?

DANIELLE No. Just the kid's research. *(shines flashlight on the research)* What are *you* doing here?

JULIA Just wandering.

DANIELLE Nobody just "wanders" down to the Flats. You have to have a reason to come.

Pause.

You're thinking about her, no?

Silence.

I thought you might want to talk about it or something. *(after a beat)* Pretty funny about that kid, eh? Thinking she saw Champlain like that? She really did, too. She started pointing and shouting and– *(a thought)* Hey! Come on! *(takes JULIA by the hand)*

JULIA What are you doing?

DANIELLE Come on!

CHAMPLAIN

JULIA *(to the commission)* We drove to the statue of Champlain that looks out over the Ottawa River, and the city crowded round its shore.

DANIELLE I used to come here all the time!

She takes out a flask. Drinks, passes it to JULIA. They share the flask.

Oh no! He's gone!

JULIA	Who?
DANIELLE	My little Indian! I don't believe it. He used to be right here, a statue of a little Indian, right here at Champlain's feet, hunched down like this, huh? *(She demonstrates.)* Staring, like this. *(She demonstrates.)* Where did he go, my little Indian? I used to come here, when I was lonely, or afraid, when I needed an answer. I'd look out over this place, I'd think, "it's not a city, it's a town, and I'm stuck in it. Supposed to be for English and French. It's not for either." So I'd put my arm around my little Indian, you know? I'd say, "what should I do? Where should I go?"
JULIA	And what would he say?
DANIELLE	Nothing. He'd just keep staring. *(She laughs.)* But I never knew what he was staring at. *(beat)* This is the way he came, uh? Champlain. Upriver, fighting against the current. The Algonquins, they guided him, showed him the way in. Now there's hardly any left. No one to guide us.
CHAMPLAIN	This waterfall makes such a noise in this basin that it can be heard for more than two leagues away.
	JULIA looks up at CHAMPLAIN. DANIELLE looks at JULIA, then follows her gaze up.
DANIELLE	Hey, what's he holding, anyway? I always wondered.
JULIA	An astrolabe.
DANIELLE	Oh yeah?
JULIA	Yeah. Except – you know what? It's upside down.

DANIELLE	Yeah? No wonder he got lost. Good to be lost sometimes. *(beat)* Getting cold. This wind, uh? Still early. I'm meeting some friends in Hull. Drink. Dance. I feel like doing something crazy. You ever feel like that, Julia?
JULIA	Have a good time.
DANIELLE	Yeah. See you in the morning.

> *DANIELLE goes. JULIA looks out at the river.*

CHAMPLAIN	Look up there. We are so small, are we not? You know, on the way over here one time, it must have been, I don't know, 1610, 1611, somewhere in there, I took out my astrolabe, looking for the North Star. Well, this night, when I looked up, a thought creeped into my head. It said, "Samuel, it's pretty incredible, you know. You've sailed all over the world, you've accomplished so much in so short a time, and yet, how little you've done." Look up there. All those worlds to conquer, all those stars to name. Madame, as I looked up that night, I wished the skies would open, and show me the way to heaven. Ah well. I can't even find the way to China. But perhaps I might find the way – to your heart.

> *They kiss. CHAMPLAIN becomes BILL, years earlier.*

JULIA	Well. That's a surprise. I thought we came out here to look at shooting stars.
BILL	No, we came out here to neck and generally fondle each other. But if you want to get back to the party, and watch a bunch of drunken engineering students dry hump a blow-up doll, by all means.

> *JULIA leans back, looks up.*

> *(taking out a flask)* Have a nip?

JULIA   No thanks.

> *They look.*

BILL   *(singing)* "But the sea is wide, and I can't swim over / And neither have I wings to fly. / I wish I could find me / A handsome boatman"–

JULIA   Handy. It's a handy boatman.

BILL   This one's handsome. *(looking up)* Anything?

JULIA   Too much glare.

BILL   Can I tell you a secret?

JULIA   You may.

BILL   I'm crazy about you.

JULIA   Yeah? What's the secret?

BILL   You're funny. Okay, how about this: I'm gonna marry you.

JULIA   Is that right?

BILL   I can tell the future. We're gonna have kids.

JULIA   Is this before or after we graduate?

BILL   Yes.

JULIA   Got it all worked out, have you?

BILL   It's written in the stars.

JULIA	"Gaseous objects made luminous by nuclear explosions." I don't care for prophecy.
BILL	For every shooting star we see tonight, we're gonna have one kid.
JULIA	What if this glorious future of yours isn't written in the stars but in the wind?
BILL	Translation.
JULIA	I've been accepted into the Urban Planning department at U of T.
BILL	I didn't know you applied.
JULIA	I didn't want to have to live down the rejection. And now I don't.
BILL	So you're just gonna quit the programme.
JULIA	Mine eyes have been opened. I've been reading Jane Jacobs. *The Death and Life of Great American Cities.* Revolutionary ideas.
BILL	"Down with cars! Up with people!"
JULIA	I love a man who reduces progressive thinking to slogans.
BILL	The revolution needs a slogan.
JULIA	Not that one. She's not against cars. She's against bad planning. These modern Utopias—Garden City, Radiant City—with their promises of vast parkland, uniformity, a living death – they have to be fought. I want to be part of the fight.
BILL	Why can't you fight it with an engineering degree?

JULIA	Someone else can build bridges; I want to build communities.
BILL	Speaking of slogans. Anyway, the sisterhood'll never forgive you for quitting.
JULIA	The sisterhood will thank me for helping create streets they don't have to be afraid to walk down, streets their kids can play on, watched by their neighbours, people they know and trust, streets in constant use, no dark corners, no blind alleys–
BILL	Yeah yeah, and a grocery on every corner.
JULIA	–streets you can walk down where people look you in the eye, smile, strike up a conversation.
BILL	There are streets like that. They're near insane asylums.
JULIA	Nuts to you. I don't see our downtowns go the way of American ones.
BILL	You can't force people to live in the city. You're living in another time, Julia. Things aren't like that anymore.
JULIA	But they can be.
BILL	Look, I admire your resolve. It's just–
JULIA	I think you mean my "pluck," don't you? You admire my pluck? Let me clear up your confusion. Drop the patronizing tone.
BILL	Right. You're right.
JULIA	Now congratulate me.
BILL	I was just about to. How long's the course?

JULIA	Two years.
BILL	When do you start?
JULIA	Next semester. Hey. "It's written in the stars."
BILL	Yeah.

He looks up. She doesn't.

Julia! I just saw one!

JULIA	Where?
BILL	Right over the Parliament Buildings! Keep looking! Fantastic! I've never... wait, there's bound to be another one...

They look.

JULIA Just the one, I guess. Is that enough for you? *(to the commission)* Danielle had left Robyn's research behind. I began to look through it. She had drawn a cross-section of the land, and carefully written, in small, delicate handwriting, the geological names and dates of each layer beneath the earth. All those "zoics" I could never commit to memory in high school. I turned the page, and saw images of Champlain. Next was the first survey of the area, a crude map drawn by one John Stegmann.

At last I came to an aerial photograph, taken not long ago. Not of the Flats alone, but of the city. I stared so long, and maybe it was the wine, or the hour, or both, but the page began to shimmer, come alive.

I felt as though I were flying, sailing through the air, over houses, trees, the tallest buildings in the city. A city I had never left. My world. I leaned into the wind, swooping and diving. I saw the hospital in which I'd been born, the home in which I'd grown up, the home in which I'd been living. I saw the buildings in which I'd been educated, and married, where I worked and where I played. Here was my life, contained as it was, on a piece of paper. I could see it, playing itself out. I came at last to the train station, where I'd said my last goodbye to my daughter, and with a quick hug, a wave from the window, I watched the train, moving north, on the paper, until it disappeared off the edge of the map. Then the train returned, but only he was on it. His face, his arms, reaching out, not taken. She was taken by the river, the river now flowing on paper, river water on my hands, no, not water, tears, my tears, a flood of tears that drowned this city, as it had been millions of years ago, and there, there, on the paper before me, I watched as the waters subsided, as land appeared, as trees grew, the tallest pines and maples, reaching, soaring for warmth.

STEGMANN

JULIA   *(to the commission)* I opened my eyes. I was on the Flats again. I don't know how I got there. I must have walked, but had no memory of walking. All around me were trees. The first rays of dawn slanted through the leaves. I tilted back my head, and saw the trunks of pines and maples stretch in an unbroken line towards the sky. I heard something snap behind me. I turned, but it was only me. Seven years old, in a pretty summer dress. I picked up a branch from the base of a tree, and handed it to myself. I thought about what Robyn had said, about using branches to measure an acre. And I wondered if we measured our memories in the same way. Drew lines through our past, roughed out roads and blocks?

I found a twig and stuck it in the ground to mark the first corner. I then took up the branch, and began to lay it end to end. One... two...

John STEGMANN appears, walking along and writing in a diary.

STEGMANN   Black ash, pine, some cedar and hemlock.

JULIA   I turned and saw a young man, his head down, writing in a notebook as he walked along.

STEGMANN   Maple, basswood, some elm and– *(seeing JULIA)* A woman. Alone?

JULIA nods.

Lovely lady. The forest is no place for you. It is very dangerous here. Very dark and – dangerous. Luckily for you, you are in the presence of a soldier and a gentleman. Well. Ex-soldier. Stegmann. John Stegmann.

JULIA   Pleasure to meet you.

STEGMANN   Ya, I am with the Office of the Surveyor General. I am here to stake out four townships. Here is a good spot. Bit of a tedious swamp, but these trees will provide shelter and building material. And the waterfall is an excellent source of power. The troops will settle here, as payment for their services.

JULIA   You're German.

STEGMANN   Born and bred.

JULIA	I thought you'd be British.
STEGMANN	The point is, I am in their employ. I Iave been ever since I left my little town of Hesse. How I miss it. Saying goodbye to my mother and father – and Greta – lovely Greta. But a man must go where the work is. I joined the British army to fight these rebels in America, you know.
JULIA	A mercenary, then.
STEGMANN	We are all mercenaries, fraulein. It is "fraulein," isn't it? I don't mean to pry.
JULIA	I'm not married if that's what you're asking.
STEGMANN	No need to explain. I have many spinster aunties and they are perfectly happy. They knit. Do you come here to commune with nature?
JULIA	I'm doing a survey.
STEGMANN	But that's quite impossible. This is my area.
JULIA	The survey is for myself.
STEGMANN	Ah. Where are your instruments?
JULIA	I'm using this stick.
STEGMANN	Stick! Ha ha! This is very amusing to me.
JULIA	It's how the Germans did it.
STEGMANN	Which Germans? None that I know. In any case, if you're going to conduct a survey—an accurate one—you need a circumferentor. Yes? A rifle site attached to a circular plate. You set it up, squat down— excuse—then send your axemen down the line of sight, taking the chain with them,

playing it out one link at a time, like our memories, ya? It takes a long time, you know, because the axemen have to cut down the trees and all this. But they're very good at it, these savages. Strong, you know? They're here somewhere. They went to the river, I think, to throw tobacco. The point is, when the chain is – mm–

JULIA

Taut.

STEGMANN

Ya, good, "taut." *(He writes it down.)* "Taut." Then you wave to your axemen, like this– *(He demonstrates.)* –to get them to move left or right until they're back on the compass heading. When they are, you tell them to stick in the picket, in the ground. And so you have a line. And then on to the next, and the next, until a grid is formed. The British, they like things nice and straight you know. That's how they keep their subjects in line.

JULIA

Nice book.

STEGMANN

Ya. Surveying is such a tedious way to make a living. To keep myself sane, I write down my thoughts and observations. Please. *(He hands her the book.)* I never seem to have enough pencils. I'm down to my last one at the moment.

JULIA

(reading from his notebook) Monday, April 12, 1794: "Procured the necessaries. Very good going." Tuesday, April 13: "Ran the North Limit." Wednesday: "Rained all day." Friday: "Very good going." Sunday: "Lay still this day." "Lay still this day." That's lovely.

STEGMANN

Very kind.

> *Piano music is heard. A bar.*
> *STEGMANN still has his accent,*
> *is now PETER.*

JULIA	*(looking around)* I can't imagine what's keeping Bill.
PETER	This gives us more time to get better acquainted. You said you also came to this profession by chance.
JULIA	Not chance, exactly, Peter. I was going to go into urban planning.
PETER	And?
JULIA	The summer before I was to begin my studies, I got pregnant.
PETER	This happens many many times. We sacrifice our dreams to economic need. But now that your daughter's in school, is there any reason you shouldn't get back into planning?
JULIA	I may get back to it. But at the moment I'm studying to become a surveyor.
PETER	This is a job for technicians, my dear, not someone of your intelligence.
JULIA	You'd be surprised.
PETER	The point is, do you want to be the musician, or the recording engineer?
JULIA	You Europeans have such a way of putting things.
PETER	And you North Americans are very glib. You seem incapable of having a serious conversation about yourselves. Why do you think this is?
JULIA	I don't know, but I'm guessing you have a theory.

PETER   It's because you have no idea who you are.
             You live in a country that was created not
             out of nationalistic fervor or some other
             sort of revolutionary ideal, but to serve the
             needs of your British masters.

JULIA   Yes, you Germans understand Imperialism
             very well.

PETER   Mere amateurs compared to the British.
             You were created in order to facilitate,
             indeed to justify, the pillaging of the new
             world. What is your founding myth?
             Where is your she-wolf, your tea party,
             your Magna Carta, your storming of the
             Bastille? A nation that has no greatness to
             look back on, will never become a great
             nation. Nor will it ever produce a great
             people.

JULIA   We're working on it.

PETER   Who is working? Planners, artists,
             architects are the ones who imagine best
             what a country might become. But your
             planners are functionaries. And your artists
             are so parochial. They seem incapable of
             imagining a world beyond that which can
             be set in a kitchen, or a farmhouse.
             Everything you do is a celebration of
             the ordinary. It's not surprising that you
             produce no geniuses, no Bach, no
             Beethoven, no Bismarck–

JULIA   No Hitler.

PETER   He was Austrian. Let's be clear on this. But
             let me come back to you.

JULIA   Oh, I can't wait.

PETER   You and your husband have been
             struggling for some time. This is all about
             to end. When Bill arrives, I am going to tell

him that we have decided to hire him.
Yes. Soon, he is going to be travelling
throughout the world, working on projects
for us. This will solve your financial
problems, but it will also create new ones.
That is why I am going to suggest the
family relocate to Europe. Believe me, I
know from experience how a job such as
this, with all its travelling and so, can put
pressures on a family. And from what I
understand of your daughter—Bill talks of
her all the time—she will absolutely fall in
love with Europe.

Pause.

Of course, we want to help you, as well,
Julia. There are any number of excellent
planning and design schools in Europe.
We would pay the tuition, and see to it that
you were employed by a top firm once you
graduate.

JULIA   Our families are here. I couldn't imagine a
change like that.

PETER   Naturally, you'll want to think it over. But
I do hope you will accept.

The music cuts out.

JULIA   I should have gone. Bill tried desperately to
convince me. I told him I couldn't do that
to our daughter. But what if I'd gone? Then
they wouldn't have gone away together,
just the two of them.

STEGMANN   Fate, Julia. She had come to the end of the
chain. You understand? Her chain was taut.
Some of us, we have chains that stretch
many links, long long. And some–

*He shows a small distance between his
hands.*

I don't want you to think I am not feeling your daughter's death. The point is, you cannot agonize so over this. You had no control over it. You know, one day, I set out on a ship – the good ship *Speedy*. All of a sudden comes a terrible storm, the ship capsizes, down we go, down, down, down. Fate. Oh no. I have upset you. Of course, speaking of another drowning incident. Sometimes I have no brain in my head, you know.

JULIA   *(counting out paces)* 27... 28... 29...

STEGMANN   Can I tell you something? When I was, when it was near the end there, and so, I began to feel at peace you know, in the water. I felt like I was being taken home, Julia. Home. *(writes in his journal)* October 8, 1804. Lay still this day.

                His axeman appears.

                Ah, my axeman. You know, these Algonquins, they believe that when they die, they will be reborn. Here. In this spot. *(He hands her the pencil.)* Lovely lady, it would be a most happy mercenary you would be making by accepting this gift. To remember me.

JULIA   It's your last one.

STEGMANN   That's all one wants, from the living. To be remembered.

                STEGMANN goes. The axeman is now TOM.

TOM   Morning.

JULIA   Morning.

TOM   Tom.

JULIA	Yes. How goes the scouting?
TOM	Pretty good. Gonna check out the river today. You know, for the canoe chase?
JULIA	Right.
TOM	Smoke?
JULIA	Thanks.
TOM	Light?
JULIA	I quit.
TOM	What's with the stick?
JULIA	Oh. I'm measuring out an acre.
TOM	Cutbacks?
JULIA	What?
TOM	What happened to the fancy thingummy you were looking through yesterday?
JULIA	Oh. That's coming later. This is just – well I'm not sure. I found it this morning. Must have been blown here in the windstorm.
TOM	From where?
JULIA	Well, that's a question. Anyway, I should get ready for work. We only got in a half day yesterday.
TOM	Be lucky to get that much in today. Gonna storm.
JULIA	*(looking up)* How can you tell?
TOM	Weather Channel. Have a better one.

Starts to go.

JULIA	Hey, wait a second. Yesterday, when I saw you here, you were talking about... there was a partridge... are you Algonquin?
TOM	Nope.
JULIA	Oh.
TOM	Don't look so disappointed. I'm Cree.
JULIA	No, it's just: is that a sign?
TOM	Yes. It's a sign that I'm Cree.
JULIA	No. The partridge. You said something about – you said a name.
TOM	Constant Penency.
JULIA	Right. What did you mean by that?
TOM	These were his hunting grounds.
JULIA	He was a real person.
TOM	Sure, fought for the British. Then he watched his land being settled. But he was an understanding sort. Instead of blasting people off, he sent nice petitions to the King, asking for a little of it back. Just a little. Signed his name with the image of a partridge.
JULIA	Did he get his land back?
TOM	Nope. That's why I like to think that's him. Still asking.
	DAVIDSON, DANIELLE and ROBYN arrive. DAVIDSON whistles.
DAVIDSON	Christ, it's *hot*. I swear to god, I'm gonna melt, and it's only nine o'clock. This is the craziest weather I've– Hey, Julia.

JULIA	Davidson.
TOM	Morning.
DAVIDSON	How – you doing?
TOM	*(to JULIA)* See you around.
JULIA	I'd like to hear more.
TOM	Trailer's right over there. *(looking at watch, then at DAVIDSON)* Ooh, I'm late for the bingo game.

> TOM *goes.*

DAVIDSON	Going native, are we?
JULIA	Morning, Danielle.
DANIELLE	Hi. How was your night?
JULIA	Earth shattering. Robyn, how you feeling today?
ROBYN	Great!
JULIA	Uh huh. *(handing over the research)* You left this here.
ROBYN	Ohmigod! I was looking for it everywhere! Thank you so so so much.
JULIA	Yeah. Look, if it starts to heat up again, you're going home.
ROBYN	I'll be fine, really. No more trips to the river, promise.
JULIA	You'll be going home.
DAVIDSON	What are you, her mother?

JULIA	*(to the commission)* Our work continued. The group was somewhat more subdued than the day before. Danielle had stayed out all night, drowning her sorrows; Davidson was wilting in the heat. And I, I found myself wanting to be alone on the acre. *(to DANIELLE)* Move left, Danielle.
ROBYN	*(to DAVIDSON)* What are you working on?
DAVIDSON	Sketches. *(privately)* Wanna see 'em?
	DANIELLE puts the rod down, hits something hard.
JULIA	Problem?
DANIELLE	There's a rock or something. *The others gather round. ROBYN looks through her research.* No, not a rock. Concrete.
JULIA	Maybe a lane way?
DANIELLE	Look, you can see where it's coming through the weeds, here, and here.
ROBYN	It's a staircase. *(She shows them the map.)* See? We're standing right here. There was a tavern here. The Duke House. This must have been the entrance.
JULIA	Alright, we'll have to mark it with a pencil for now.
ROBYN	They must have left the foundations.
DANIELLE	Of what?
JULIA	Danielle?

ROBYN	There were homes here, stores – a whole neighbourhood. Working class. A few Irish, but mainly French.
DAVIDSON	That was a long time ago kid. *(Irish)* "When the earth was green."
JULIA	Danielle – the rod.

> *DANIELLE holds the rod straight, but gets engrossed in the conversation, and the rod swings to one side. JULIA gives up, walks over to the group.*

ROBYN	Not that long. Only about forty years. The government wanted to build offices here, so they moved everyone out, and tore down all the buildings.
DAVIDSON	It's called expropriation.
DANIELLE	It's called screw the French.
DAVIDSON	Oh please.
DANIELLE	And the working class.
DAVIDSON	That has nothing to do with what happened here.
DANIELLE	You telling me if it was a bunch of rich Anglos with their big mansions here the government would have kicked them out, knocked down their homes?
DAVIDSON	Well, duh, no, cause it wouldn't have been a slum then.
DANIELLE	"Slum," why, cause the people who lived here were poor?
DAVIDSON	No, cause the people who lived here lived in shitty decrepit unsafe–

DANIELLE	Right, right.
DAVIDSON	–houses which – just listen – you asked me and I'm gonna tell you. I mean let's not get all sentimental about this. This area was decaying. It just wasn't safe. There was a junk yard at one end of the street – kids would go play in there. A lumber yard somewhere around here, a paint factory, god knows what else. And not a park in sight. I mean is that the kind of neighbourhood you'd want your kids to grow up in? You ask me, the people who lost their houses were better off in the long run. Not only did they get fair value, they probably got more than would have if they'd–
DANIELLE	Spoken like a true bureaucrat.
DAVIDSON	I'll tell you what, you find me someone who used to live here, ask him if he'd like to come back, what do you think he'd say?
DANIELLE	*But there's nothing to come back to, you asshole.*
DAVIDSON	Oh go to Hull.
DANIELLE	Maudite, tete carré.
DAVIDSON	Bite moi! The simple, unadorned fact is that the government of the day wanted to make Ottawa a true capital. They had a vision for it, they wanted it to reflect the glory of this country.
DANIELLE	I guess that's why it's still empty.
DAVIDSON	Yeah, you know, that's the kind of attitude that keeps this country so small. You know what? If you want to be big, you gotta think big, and you gotta build big. And in five years, when this area is transformed,

yeah transformed, into a place people will want to live in, to play in, to do business in, you'll see why the government was right to do what it did.

STAN comes by.

STAN   Afternoon, folks.

DAVIDSON   Stan.

DANIELLE   Hi, Stan.

STAN   Danielle.

ROBYN   Hello.

STAN   Yes, yes, hello. Feeling better, and all that?

ROBYN   Oh much.

STAN   Good. Rain cooled things down, eh? Hello, Julia.

JULIA   Stan, brings you here?

STAN   Well, here's the thing. You people have done some marvellous work. Really, just marvellous–

DAVIDSON fake farts.

Ha ha ha! Now you knock that off! Now, look, you've put in two days of hard, hard work under very gruelling circumstances, and–

DAVIDSON fake cries on STAN's shoulder.

DAVIDSON   Thank you, thank you.

STAN   Now you stop that. The point is, I want all of you to come to the house this weekend for dinner. I'm going to order Chinese food, and we're going to have a regular old, um, time. I know it's short notice, but.... Well look, here are the directions.

He passes out bits of paper.

Did them on the computer. Nice scenic tour. Right along Richmond Road. Robyn, you'd be interested in this. The Richmond Road was created by Irish settlers. Soldiers, I think. At least that's what the agent told us when we bought– (*Seeing JULIA, he stops short.*) Well, come around seven, eh? Don't worry about bringing anything – just yourselves.

DAVIDSON   Thanks, Stan.

ROBYN   See you there, then.

DAVIDSON, DANIELLE and ROBYN go.

STAN   I um – didn't hear a yea or nay from you. I understand your not wanting to come. I mean, after what happened last night.

JULIA   Last night?

STAN   When we had drinks. I said some things. About my wife. Things which – well – your reaction, I was somewhat stupified by it. I spent the night trying to figure out what I might have said that would set you off like that. Then I realized, I put it together, you see – you thought I was using the story of my wife's death to, oh what's the phrase...

JULIA   Get into my pants?

STAN   Well. Yes. But I wasn't doing that. I would never do that. I mean, I – but not by –

dammit. I had it all worked out, you know. If only the things in our head could just sort of come out—pop!—like that, eh? Yes. That breeze is nice.

Pause.

Remembering the good things, that's the hard part. It's the terrors that come so easily to mind, god knows why. Her final moments, seeing her helplessness. Maybe we don't think we deserve to remember the happy occasions. Just now, for example, I'm recalling a walk we took, right here, right along that path by the river. We started at home, and just kept walking along the road. I can remember the wind that day, and the, good lord, silly little things, a, what do you call it, dragonfly, yes, with radiant blue uhh–

JULIA   Wings.

STAN   Wings, yes, landing on the path, then taking off, landing. "Little helicopter" she said. We talked of children that day. Yes. Right along that path. Do you know something? I think that must be why I came by just now. Yes, yes, I'm sure that's it.

JULIA   Of course. Stan. You're a nice fella.

STAN   Oh.

JULIA   I wasn't thinking what you thought I was thinking.

STAN   No?

Pause.

JULIA   Five years ago, Stan, I lost my daughter. She drowned in the Ottawa River, about a

hundred miles north of here. A camping
trip with her father. They never found her
body. We never had a proper funeral. My
husband left me a year later. I found her
diary. The last entry read, "going north,"
exclamation point, exclamation point. For
about a year, I fell asleep and woke up
seeing in my mind her beautiful fingers
gripping the pen that traced those two
strokes. I heard her scream and I heard her
cry and I heard her call for me.

    Pause.

I was on a survey. A subdivision it was.
There was a cell phone call for me. My
husband. That's all I remember. The rest is
black as night. I wasn't there. That's what
I was thinking about, Stan, when you were
telling me about your wife, about how you
found a way to go on.

**FIFTH
COMMISSIONER**
    *Naturally, Miss Wright, we're sympathetic.
Still, you might have asked to be reassigned.*

**SECOND
COMMISSIONER**
    Did you ask to be reassigned?

JULIA
    *(to the COMMISSIONER) No. I began to
think that I had been sent to the Flats for a
reason. A reason beyond the merely technical.
There were others in the department whom Stan
might have sent, but it was me he chose.*

    And so I began to measure the second side.

    TOM approaches.

TOM
    All alone?

JULIA
    Just packing up.

TOM
    Crazy weather.

JULIA	Nutty.
TOM	So, about the stick. I saw you flipping it over and over just now. What's the idea?
JULIA	No idea. I just – oh!
TOM	What?
JULIA	I just felt a drop of rain.
TOM	You better get inside.
JULIA	I'm alright. I like the rain.
TOM	You're not gonna like it when you're soaked to the bone. Supposed to pour. We're talking torrential rainfall. You're welcome to sit in the trailer, wait it out. I'll show you my petitions. You know, the ones Constant Penency signed. You said you wanted to hear more, didn't you?

A crack of thunder.

Gotta be a sign.

They run off.

CONSTANT PENENCY

Inside the trailer.

JULIA	Ah! Hurry up, hurry up!

Cell phone rings. He reaches for it.

TOM	Scuse me. (*He answers.*) Yeah... hey... I'm in Ottawa... mm hm...

As he speaks, JULIA looks around the trailer.

...right... what's the role... what kind of
Indian?... Number Three... nuts, I had my
heart set on Number Two... alright, e-mail
me the sides. See ya.

He switches off.

JULIA   Nice place.

TOM   Thanks. You pay taxes?

JULIA   Sure.

TOM   Then *thanks.* You helped pay for it. They
               used to give us beads and axes. Now we
               get trailers and arts grants.

JULIA   You live in this thing?

TOM   Pretty much.

JULIA   Who's this?

TOM   My mother.

JULIA   How old is she here?

TOM   Twenty, twenty-one.

JULIA   You've got her eyes.

               Pause.

               When did she die?

TOM   Did I say she died?

JULIA   No, but. I guess I just assumed. Am
               I wrong?

TOM   Nope.

JULIA   Well. Did you want me to think I was
               wrong?

TOM	Nope.
JULIA	What did you want me to think?
TOM	Nothing.
JULIA	Maybe I should go.
TOM	No, stay. I just couldn't remember telling you, that's all.

Pause.

JULIA	Is this the rewind button? *(beat)* Who's this?
TOM	My mother.
JULIA	How old is she here?
TOM	Twenty, twenty-one. People say I've got her eyes.
JULIA	What do you say?
TOM	I say she taught me to see.
JULIA	Bravo.
TOM	You know those people who say, "live everyday like it's your last"? She said, "live everyday like it's your first." Be full of wonder. She died about a year ago. Not the best year of my life. My series was cancelled. So was my marriage. *(pointing to a picture)* My ex.
JULIA	She's white.
TOM	*(beat; looks at photo as though stunned)* Oh my god– *(looks more closely)* I knew there was something about her I didn't like.

Pause.

JULIA	I need to know something. I need you to – I have questions.
TOM	About Penency.
JULIA	My little partridge.
TOM	Truth is, there's not a lot to tell. If it weren't for the petitions, we wouldn't know much at all.
JULIA	Isn't that funny.
TOM	How?
JULIA	If he hadn't had to write the petitions, there'd be no record of him.
TOM	He may have been happier in obscurity.
JULIA	Have you got any wine?
TOM	Nope. Don't drink. Wanna smoke a joint?
JULIA	Ooh. Makes me paranoid. Sure.
	He takes out a joint. They smoke through the following.
TOM	Okay. The Ballad of Constant Penency. Sing along at home. Born in 1786. Fought for the Brits in the War of 1812. After the war, he went home. To hunt. Deer, beaver, fish.
JULIA	Where exactly?
TOM	Didn't have an "exactly." "Around here."
JULIA	No fixed borders.
TOM	Nothing drawn on a map. No need for surveyors.
JULIA	You sharing that?

TOM	1830. By now, Constant is a Great Chief.
JULIA	What's that mean?
TOM	Means he was pretty good at it. He also files his first petition. He– *(holds up the joint)* reefers – to a stretch of land south of the Ottawa River, at the top of the Rideau. That's, what, a couple of miles thataway?
JULIA	Thataway.
TOM	Right. He says his lands are being ruined because of incursions being made by–
JULIA	"Incursions."
TOM	Settlements. 19th century Eurotrash. Soldiers and their families, who'd been given land grants. The ultimate cousins from hell. "Y'all mind if we bunk here awhile?" 200 years later, they're still sleeping in our beds.
JULIA	Christ, this stuff is strong.
TOM	Yup.
JULIA	Okay. So he writes this petition. What happens?
TOM	You know how I said he was a Great Chief?
JULIA	Yeah.
TOM	The Brits make him a Grand Chief.
JULIA	He got the corner office.
TOM	Nope. Just a better rifle, warmer blanket. Four years later, he's back to ask for a small piece of land on the south side of the river. Didn't get that, either. Last we hear of him, he's 90 years old, living on a small pension,

cared for by his daughter 'til the day he dies. In one lifetime, he'd seen a way of life disappear before his eyes. When I heard about him, I knew I had to use him in my movie.

JULIA   Yes, for the symbolism.

TOM   Hell no. For the realism. Unless you think it isn't happening anymore. The movie asks the question: how—not when, but how—will we get our land back? By talking? More petitions? Or action? Blowing off steam? Or blowing up dams?

JULIA   And the answer?

TOM   My mother, she was involved in a land claim. For 20 years, she sat across the table from politicians of one suit or another. For 20 years, they argued the same points. But let's face it, the men who were sent to talk represented the will of the people, and the people don't want to see land claims settled, not if they're to our benefit. My mother, who gave me eyes, refused to see that. And as she lay dying, she said to me, her artist son, "tell our stories. That's how we'll get it back." *(beat)* You know, I didn't show you those petitions.

               Pause. He gets a petition. He reads.

               "Good mother–"

JULIA   Mother?

TOM   Queen Victoria. This is the last petition Penency sent. "I cannot cross the great Lake to talk to you for my canoe is too small, and I am old and weak. You cannot hear my voice across the Great Waters. I therefore send this Wampum and Paper talk to tell the Queen I am in trouble. My people are in trouble. Good mother, I have seen upwards of a thousand Moons. When I was young, I had plenty: now I am poor and sickly. I am like the beast of the forest that has no shelter. I lie down on the snow, and cover myself with the boughs of the trees. My people are poor. Poor for ever. All these woods once ours. Now we cannot cut a Tree to warm our Wigwam unless the White Man please. We look to you. We hope in you. If you will promise to come, I will have my little fish ready drawn from the water, that you may taste of the food which sustains me."

"Good mother, listen to the prayers of your children. Let us not perish. Your Indian Children love you. My Head and my Heart shall go to One above for you."

Pause.

Good mother. Here are daisies. Clover.

JULIA	No.
TOM	Don't be frightened, mother. I sent for you, to come to this place. To let me go.
JULIA	I can't.
TOM	Two souls, mother. One to travel to the other side, to wait for you. The other to remain here, to be reborn. In rock and tree, in breeze and fire. In bird and animal.
TOM & VOICE OF LOUISE	I want to be reborn, mother. Let me go.
JULIA	I can't.
LOUISE	I hate you. I hate you!
JULIA	I can't.

LOUISE	I'm so lonely, mother. I am made to wander alone. I want to go. Please let me go. Please let me go.
	Pause.
JULIA	What was that stuff, peyote or something?
TOM	Pretty strong.
JULIA	I gotta lie down. *(She does.)* I was here once. With my family. A perfect day. A lovely day. A white partridge landed at our feet. What does it mean, when a white animal comes into a territory?
TOM	Algonquin. They thought it meant bad luck. I kinda figure they made that one up after the Europeans got here. They brought all kinds of bad luck.
JULIA	And were welcomed, with open arms.
	A pause. He lies down with her.
TOM	Now how about you telling me something?
JULIA	Nothing to tell.
TOM	What is it with you wasps anyway? A lifetime of hurt and it's always, "I'm fine. How are *you?* Look at those clouds. We'd better not go sailing. I know! Let's make jam."
JULIA	I was never very good at "let's share a secret."
TOM	Alright. Then how about telling me something about your job.
JULIA	Surveying? Please. I'd rather share jam recipes.

TOM	Well let's make it interesting. Let's say your body is the earth. How would you survey it?

Pause.

JULIA	Start with a base line.
TOM	Where?
JULIA	You choose.
TOM	Mm. How about – here.
JULIA	Good a spot as any.
TOM	What now?
JULIA	Send your – rodman – down your line of sight.
TOM	(*walking his fingers along her body.*) "Dumdeedumdeedum – Nice day for a survey – kinda hilly around here – dumdeedumdeedum–"
JULIA	Then you wave to your rodman, to get him to move left – or right – to make sure he's on the correct lo-o-o-ongitude. When he reaches the survey point, you wave to him to stop.
TOM	And then?
JULIA	He plants his stake in the ground. The next morning he's gone and you never hear from him again.
TOM	But here's the thing. If you're here, and the rodman's here, you can't see him. These lines don't make any sense.
JULIA	No.

TOM	*(seeing her c-section scar)* And what's this line?
	She pushes her shirt down, sits up. Pause.
JULIA	When your mother died, what did you do? At the funeral, I mean.
TOM	Well. It lasted four days. We fasted. Danced. Prayed. Let her go.
JULIA	What does that mean? "Let her go?"
TOM	Means you don't try to control her spirit – you let her go on. So she can be reborn. See?
JULIA	How do you know when the spirit leaves?
TOM	Spirit's breath. When breath is gone, the spirit's gone. It hovers over the body, waits for our blessing. Goes.
JULIA	And is reborn. Here. In this spot.

ACT TWO

LEBRETON

JULIA

(to the commission) I did not sleep very well that night. Hardly at all, in fact. I kept thinking about the acre, about the people who'd been and lived and died there. It had never meant much to me. But it was beginning to.

At dawn, I wrote a quick note to Tom, slipped out of the trailer, and began to measure the third side. One... two... three...

LEBRETON and ELIZABETH LeBreton appear.

LEBRETON

Bloody 'ell! It's a swamp! Look at my shoes! I just bought 'em, too. Half a crown they cost me.

ELIZABETH

Now now, Uncle. Soon you will be able to buy all the shoes you wish. *(looking off)* Girls, get out of the muck please.

LEBRETON

You really fink the government's gonna wanna buy it?

ELIZABETH

Uncle it was you who heard of Lord Dalhousie's plans for this area. He wants to put a canal here, and when he discovers that we own the land, he shall have no choice but to purchase it from us – no matter the price.

LEBRETON

Clever girl. *(seeing JULIA)* Oh 'ello madame. You wif the government?

JULIA

In a manner of speaking.

LEBRETON

(aside to ELIZABETH) Indirect response. Definitely wif the government. *(to JULIA)* What department?

JULIA	National Capital Commission.
LEBRETON	I am not familiar wif this particular agency. Does it deal wif land acquisition?
JULIA	In part.
LEBRETON	Well that's the part that interests me. Allow me to introduce myself. Captain John LeBreton, veteran of the War of 1812, including the notorious battle of Lundy's Lane, where I lost half my... brain... and now infected with the entrepreneurial spirit of the age. I am the progenitor of these lands, and–
ELIZABETH	Proprietor, uncle.
LEBRETON	That's right, and these are my daughters.
ELIZABETH	Nieces.
LEBRETON	As you wish. This one's Emily, the youngest of the brood.
EMILY	Hello.
JULIA	How do you do, Emily?
EMILY	Very nicely, I may say and thank you for asking, you're a very kind lady and perhaps one day I may–
LEBRETON	That's enough. They do go on a bit. I'd'a preferred sons, they don't yammer on so bloody much.
EMILY	Nephews.
LEBRETON	Who said that?
THE NIECES	Her – was not! – get back in line.

ELIZABETH turns and makes farting noise to the sisters.

LEBRETON   Now, here we have Louisa.

LOUISA   Pleasure, I'm sure.

JULIA   And your age?

LOUISA   It is ill-advised to reveal one's age, and ill-mannered to ask it.

LEBRETON   Oh you shall pay an heavy price for that remark, my darling. Now where's Jane?

JANE   Allo. I'm 14.

LEBRETON   A real scrapper this one. Come on, then, show me what you got. *(He boxes with her, she smashes him in the gut; he doubles over in pain.)* That's a girl. Right, here's Sophia.

SOPHIA   Very nice to meet you.

JULIA   How old are you, Sophia?

SOPHIA   Why, eleven missus.

JULIA   Eleven. Are you in school?

SOPHIA   Well, I'd like to go but–

LEBRETON   I fink you'd best not pursue that line of questioning. The girls is helping me in my business endeavours. That way, when I die–

THE NIECES   No uncle – don't speak like that – you musn't, you mustn't–

LEBRETON   Now, now, girls, dust to dust and all. As I was saying, I'll pass everyfing along to my daught– nieces.

ELIZABETH	Uncle, you have yet to introduce me.
LEBRETON	Right. This is Jane. No, said that.
ELIZABETH	I am Elizabeth, uncle.
LEBRETON	That's it. Well, madame, shall we get down to the business at 'and? I purchased this property at auction, from the estate of Robert Randall, for the sum of 499 pounds. Now, a little birdy informs me that the government wishes to put a canal here, and I am not one who wishes to stand in the way of progress.
JULIA	You're a speculator.
LEBRETON	That remark carries certain unpleasant connotations. Is it a bargaining position?
JULIA	I think you should set some land aside for Constant Penency.
LEBRETON	Constant penance? Once in the land is in government 'ands, it may do what it pleases, and if that includes putting up a Catholic Church, it makes no difference to me. I am certainly no anti-Papist.
JULIA	I'm not Catholic.
LEBRETON	What are you then?
JULIA	Agnostic.
LEBRETON	What's that?
JULIA	I'm not sure.
ELIZABETH	Uncle, Constant Penan*cy* is a native hunter.
LEBRETON	Where is he?
ELIZABETH	He flits about.

LEBRETON	Oh, I see. And you want me to just give him some land? Well, nothing doing, lady, and let me tell you why – wif a song.

British music hall.

They say that all of this
was native hunting land,
But that's all disappeared,
like footprints in the sand.

Of course they got here first–
there's no disputin' that–
but ownership of land,
comes wif a caveat:

Land belongs to him,
wot's got the right to sell,
so let us have your bid,
or let us bid farewell.

DALHOUSIE	*(emerging)* Not so fast LeBreton.
LEBRETON	Dalhowsie!
ELIZABETH	Help! Help!
DALHOUSIE	Dalhoosie – *Lord* Dalhoosie, captain general–
LEBRETON	Yeah, wull–
DALHOUSIE	–governor-in-chief of Upper—and Lower—Canada – and–
LEBRETON	You can just–
DALHOUSIE	I'm not done yet – Order of the Bath. And you, my lady, are about to be taken for one. For we are standing on government land. And no one—no matter his claim—is to interfere with the purpose to which this spot is best suited.

JULIA

And what is that?

DALHOUSIE

Why, take a look about you, my dear lady, what do you see?

JULIA

Native territory.

DALHOUSIE

Ba ha! Charming. No. It may once have been native terra-tree, but it was acquired in a transaction known as the Crawford Purchase. I shall not bore you with the details. It's in any standard book of history. In any case, my question to you was not about ownership, but about vision. Allow me to speak of mine. The trees from this great forest shall become masts for our warships in the fight 'gainst Imperial Napoleon. From the stumps shall rise a capital city, a place of warmth and splendour, the Utrecht of the Western World – and a bulwark 'gainst American invasion. And here, but a stone's throw away, we shall build a canal... a canal...

DALHOUSIE becomes BILL. He speaks into a cell phone.

BILL

It's ours?... we got the contract?... we got the contract!... ha ha ha!... jesus Peter I could... no, no thank you man... no you brought me in, nobody else was willing to take a chance on me and you... I swear to god if it wasn't for you I'd... huh?... yeah, she's here... *(to JULIA)* Peter says hi. *(into phone)* When do we start?... No I'm ready. Say the word I'm on a plane.

ELIZABETH

Three thousand pounds.

DALHOUSIE

What! That's – that's a 500 per cent profit in less than a year.

ELIZABETH

When land becomes real estate, Lord Dalhousie, it becomes valuable not for what it is, but for what it might become.

DALHOUSIE	Clever girl you have there, LeBreton. I'd like to see what she has to say when I have your pension cut off!
LEBRETON	Can he do that?
ELIZABETH	No, uncle, he's bluffing.
LEBRETON	Are you?
DALHOUSIE	Yes, dammit, you saw right through that! Well then, we shall have to settle this in court.
LEBRETON	No, no, I don't like no stinkin' courts.
DALHOUSIE	Then–
ELIZABETH	We *will* see you in court.
LEBRETON	But–
ELIZABETH	Uh uh. In court, Uncle.

LEBRETON and ELIZABETH, aside.

LEBRETON	Alright, what the hell are you finkin' about?
ELIZABETH	Simply this, Uncle. You purchased the land with Livius P. Sherwood.
LEBRETON	Yeah.
ELIZABETH	Mr Sherwood is a *judge*, Uncle.
LEBRETON	Right.
ELIZABETH	He presides over the court in which this suit will be heard.
LEBRETON	Right, I'm wif you.
ELIZABETH	Uncle – do you think this man will issue a judgment against himself?

Beat.

LEBRETON   Right, let's go over this one more time...

DALHOUSIE is BILL again.

BILL   Look. I want you to have the house. Just. When you sell it, keep the money. I mean I think, I think that's fair. You got us the down payment and–

JULIA   I'm not selling.

BILL   You're not. You're gonna stay here? Why?

JULIA   Would you go?

BILL   Julia, listen. I went back. I just–

JULIA   I don't want to hear this.

BILL   I didn't plan it, I just–

JULIA   I don't want to hear it.

And back to DALHOUSIE.

DALHOUSIE   Congratulations. It seems you have forced my hand. I shall have to build down river. Enjoy your swamp. *(to JULIA)* Madame.

LEBRETON   Oh bloody terrific. Now wot are we supposed to do?

ELIZABETH hands him a paper.

Wot's this?

ELIZABETH   A small advertisement the girls and I devised.

LEBRETON   "Land for Sale." Who the 'ell's gonna wanna buy 'ere?

ELIZABETH	What about this young lady?
LEBRETON	*(regarding JULIA)* I got the distinct impression I've met you before.
ELIZABETH	Read, Uncle.
LEBRETON	"Land for Sale, situation most beautiful and sa-sagig-sabrib–"
ELIZABETH	Salubrious, Uncle.
LEBRETON	Wot's that mean?
ELIZABETH	Good for your health.
LEBRETON	This swamp?
ELIZABETH	Read!
LEBRETON	"Situation most beautiful and – good for your 'elf – south side of the Chaudiere Falls, wif the Grand Union bridge abutting on the centre and front and leading froo the main street." *(to JULIA)* Watch your step, madame. *(reading)* "Replete wif mill sites, and for commerce no situation on the River Ottawa can equal it. Beautiful bay windows, wood floors, finished basement, close to every'fing. And, to top it off–"
	BILL enters.
BILL	Honey, have you seen the backyard?
JULIA	It's lovely. I just don't know if we can afford it.
BILL	Louise has already struck up a friendship with the girl next door. And the yard over this way is full of toys.
JULIA	*(looking at the backyard)* It's way out of our range. *(She waves.)* Sweetheart, please don't go into those bushes.

BILL	Would you leave her? Look at her. She loves it. Look – can't you just see it? Look at that tree – I'm gonna put a swing on that tree.
JULIA	You are?
BILL	Yeah! Well, some of the guys will come and help out. Think of it... the three of us out there... starry nights... we have to take it, honey.
JULIA	It's just – the money.
BILL	Okay, I wasn't gonna tell you. I made it to the next round of interviews. I think it's gonna happen. This Peter guy, he likes me, he likes my ideas. Honey, the *starting* salary is mid six figures. You can go back to school, like you always wanted. Honey, you've been saying for years you wanted your life back – well if I get this job–
LEBRETON	Right, I'll give it to you for ten pounds an acre.
ELIZABETH	No, Uncle. Fifteen.
LEBRETON	Right. Ten pounds for fifteen acres.
ELIZABETH	Ladies, a conference. (*goes aside*)
LEBRETON	They is very good to me... 'ave you a daughter?
JULIA	Had.
LEBRETON	Wot 'appened? She go off to seek her fortune like so many is doing nowadays?
JULIA	No.
LEBRETON	She marry some rich foreigner, then?

JULIA	No.
LEBRETON	Oh. Well then she musta drowned in the river. *(off her reaction)* Aw, c'mon, don't get all misty on me. Look at it this way – you had one din't you? If only for a short time. Me? All I 'ave is nieces. I mean, nieces is fine. But a daughter. That's somefing else.
JULIA	Yes.
LEBRETON	Tell you wot – why don't you take one? Yes, yes! I got five, and here you are, you ain't got one. Come on, girls, gather round, chop chop. Now look, girls, I've decided to give one of you away to this kind lady. Now, I know it shall be a difficult transition for you, going from–
THE NIECES	Pick me, pick me! – Oh, take me, Miss Wright – I got good teef – back off, strumpet – Miss Wright, of course I meant nothing by my earlier remarks – look at my teef.
JULIA	What about you, Elizabeth? You haven't said anything.
ELIZABETH	If fate should dictate that I am to be with you, Miss Wright, then nothing I have to say on the matter could possibly influence the outcome.
LEBRETON	*(shoving her forward)* Excellent choice, madame. Sorry to be so hasty and all, but I'm not feelin' too good at the moment. That little girl gave me an awful hard punch, knocked somefing loose in the intestinal tract, I fink.
JULIA	Shall I get a doctor?
LEBRETON	No, no, I don't like no stinkin' doctors. Still, I could use somefing salubrious at the

	moment. Maybe I oughta buy me land from meself.
JULIA	Here, rest yourself. *(to the NIECES)* Girls?
LEBRETON	Oh, don't bovver wif em. I do wonder how they'll get on without me. Could you look in on 'em now and again?
JULIA	Of course.
LEBRETON	Most kind a you. Gettin' dark all of a sudden.
JULIA	Is it?
LEBRETON	Yeah. Is 'at passenger pigeons I see? They say it used to take a whole day for one flock to pass overhead.
JULIA	None left now.
LEBRETON	I did alright, didn't I? I don't have no regrets. None about what I done, anyways. I got to build my ice bridge, after all. I ever tell you about my ice bridge?
JULIA	No, tell me.
LEBRETON	Well, I got to finkin' about a bridge – made of ice – to go across the Ottawa, see. I got the idea from the Indians, on account of that's how they got to this place, on a bridge of ice from Russia, see. Anyway, it worked pretty well, mine did. 'Til the spring anyway.

Pause.

Only wished I coulda stuck around long enough to watch me land grow up. I s'pose it's in good hands, though, i'n'it?

*He dies in JULIA's arms. The girls
approach.*

ELIZABETH   Gather 'round, girls. In the absence of a
priest, I shall take it upon myself to say
a few words. I commend your soul to
heaven, even though you taught us not to
believe in such a place, and that it is up to
us to create heaven here on earth. Amen.
Silent devotion. *(beat)* Let us sing.

LEBRETON rises and exits during song.

Shall we gather at the river
Where bright angel feet have trod,
With its crystal tide forever
Flowing by the throne of God.

Beat.

We're alone now. No one to guide us.
(Pause.) Would anyone like to say anything?
(SOPHIA puts up her hand.) Sophia.

SOPHIA   Can I go to school now?

ELIZABETH   Most assuredly. We are going to settle in
Toronto, which offers the finest schools in
Upper Canada, as well as stores, places of
entertainment and sidewalks. From there,
we shall administer Uncle's holdings. This
is our land now. Uncle had a vision for it,
but he was a very poor planner. Here we
are halfway through the 19th century,
British North America is filling up with
people, and yet LeBreton's Flat is little
more than a semi-vacant field.

That shall soon be taken care of. Lord
Dalhousie's fears will prove quite wrong,
you see. The Americans will not invade.
They will not need to. For we shall
welcome them with open borders. Mr.
Perley, for example, a wealthy young

successful young handsome young man
from New Hampshire, lured to our lush
virgin forests by the promise of easy access
and no protection, will set up a mill by the
falls. Mr. Perley understands the power of
water, the ebb and flow of it, the push and
pull of it, the roiling, pounding, unceasing
availability of it. He erects his mill in such
a way as to allow the logs and water to
enter from the rear, so that the motion
and turbulence of the river may drive his
magnificent saws, oh yes, mm, ever hungry
for more and more wood, so much wood,
oh!, don't stop the wood, Mr. Perley, for the
American market is *wide open*, yes, yes,
keep it coming, oh! Mr. Perley, you knotty
pine, Mr. Perley!, yes, yes, keep it coming,
rip those logs apart, yes, yes, yes, yes!

    Beat.

Well, what shall we do now, Miss Wright?
A stroll along Duke Street? Nothing more
than a boardwalk, I grant you, but progress
comes slowly round here. Now that the
trees have been cleared, the LeBreton
Flats, as we now call them, are ready to be
populated. Mainly by French and Irish mill
workers. Oh look, street lights. By the turn
of the century, there will be 4,000 people
living here, a living, breathing community,
streets in constant use, no dark corners, no
blind alleys; streets where people look you
in the eye, smile, strike up a conversation.
Good afternoon, Mr. Perley – Mrs. Perley –
I could show you the bank, or the many
shops which now carry international
goods, or—I know!—the theatre. Do
you like the theatre? There's one in this
building. It's also used as a church, school
and Orange Lodge, but once in a while a
group of touring actors from Britain or
America stop in to present popular plays.

Train whistle.

Sometimes the productions are disturbed
by the sound of a passing train, but the
actors continue on best they can. I wonder
what's playing? *(reads a poster)* "A History
of the LeBreton Flats, As Told By the People
Who Lived There." A Vaudeville! I do like a
Vaudeville! Shall we?

*They sit and watch. AUGUSTE and
MADAME DE CHAMPLAIN emerge.*

AUGUSTE   The Story of the Great Fire of 1900.
Presented by me, Auguste—not related
to—Samuel de Champlain, and my wife,
Madame de Champlain.

**MME DE
CHAMPLAIN**   *(to AUGUSTE)* I don't want to do this.

AUGUSTE   *Ferme ta guelle.* Okay, I throw that in there
about not related to Samuel de Champlain
because people always say to me, "Hey, are
you related to Samuel de Champlain?"

ELIZABETH   Well, are you?

AUGUSTE   No, no, no – but I do a hell of an
impression. *(does Samuel de Champlain)*
"Ah, yes, there we were two leagues from
the falls when we heard them – the falls.
We thought to ourselves – how the fuck
are we going to get around that? We came
ashore, and carried our boats, and–" *(his
own voice)* Anyway, goes on like that. But
you know, it was right here, right here he
set foot. He take a look around, he say,
"Not much to look at," so he go. But the
French, we stay. Well, Irish too.

They spit.

But mainly French. We build, we work for
Perley and all the lumber baron. Then,
1900, hopla! The whole thing – gone. And
now, we present to you, the story of the
Great Fire of 1900. On the Flats. Of
LeBreton.

He nods to her to start.

MME DE CHAMPLAIN	I don't want to do this.
AUGUSTE	*Tabernac*! Just say the line!
MME DE CHAMPLAIN	*(looking out)* Auguste, look, it is a fire starting in 'ull!
AUGUSTE	Where? Ah, don't worry, it won't come across the river. – Three hours later. *(He starts to sniff.)* Hey, what's that smell?
MME DE CHAMPLAIN	I don't know – I think it's – fire! Get the childrens! *(to JULIA)* Twelve kids we got. You got to have a lot of kids, you know, cause one, two they dic, they get the influenza, all kinds disease, they get run over by a tractor, fall off a cliff, whatever.
AUGUSTE	So the wife, since she's 13, she pop them out. I see some people, they have two, three childrens, you know – some, only one! They put everything into the life of this child, then, the child gone – hopla! Everything go with it. Quick, up the cliff, made of limestone, the fire, she can't climb so good.

They climb.

Are all the childrens here?

MME DE CHAMPLAIN	*(counting)* –nine, ten, eleven, twelve, thirteen.
AUGUSTE	Thirteen?
MME DE CHAMPLAIN	I had one on the way up.
AUGUSTE	Beautiful little baby. But look – our home – gone – hopla.
MME DE CHAMPLAIN	What we gonna do now?
AUGUSTE	We gonna build again! *(beat)* Thank you.
ELIZABETH	That was most interesting. Next we have the Baker Brothers, Russian Immigrants–
LOUIS & JANKOV	We certainly are!
ELIZABETH	–Who Came To Canada To Escape the Pogroms. Oh goody.
JANKOV	I'm Jankov!
LOUIS	I'm Louis!
LOUIS & JANKOV	We're the Baker Brothers!
LOUIS	Need junk? We got it!
JANKOV	We got the biggest pile of junk you ever saw.
LOUIS	What do we got, Jankov?
JANKOV	We got carburetors.
LOUIS	We got hubcaps.

JANKOV	We got exhaust pipes.
LOUIS	We got hubcaps.
JANKOV	We got pistons.
LOUIS	We got hubcaps.
JANKOV	You said that.
LOUIS	We got a lotta hubcaps.
JANKOV	What else we got?
LOUIS	Memories!
JANKOV	Sweet memories!
LOUIS	Remember the pogroms in Russia, Jankov?
JANKOV	Ah, the pogroms. You, being forced to watch your beautiful Rebekah being defiled, over and over, before having her eyes plucked out.
LOUIS	And you, returning home to find your whole family hacked to pieces, your daughter's throat slit ear to ear.
JANKOV	You know, it's like Julia says – we can't be happy...
LOUIS & **JANKOV**	We can only remember being happy.
JANKOV	But you can't live in the past, can you?
LOUIS	You gotta go on.
JANKOV	You gotta build.
LOUIS	So we built.
JANKOV	Built a junk shop.

LOUIS	The best damn junk shop in the history of junk shops.
JANKOV	I'm Jankov!
LOUIS	I'm Louis!
LOUIS & JANKOV	We're the Baker Brothers!
JANKOV	What do we got?
LOUIS	We got hazardous waste materials!
JANKOV	We got benzenes!
LOUIS	We got toluenes!
JANKOV	We got xylenes!
LOUIS	And a whole host of other aromatic compounds from the petroleum products we carelessly threw into the ground.
JANKOV	Get 'em before they leech into the ground water, destroying nervous systems and reducing sperm counts.
REBEKAH	Oh boo hoo hoo.
LOUIS	Rebekah, my blind wife, do not be upset, my sperm's fine.
REBEKAH	I'm not crying over that. It's this, a letter from the government, it don't feel too good.
LOUIS	It's a letter of expropriation.
JANKOV	Get outta here, we only do imports.
LOUIS	Schmendrick, it's from the NCC. It's here saying "This property is required as a site for government buildings and the further

redevelopment of the Ottawa River shoreline. Salubriously yours, the government."

REBEKAH   Oh boo hoo hoo.

She wanders off.

JANKOV   Why of all the nerve! After all what we been through, we finally build a home in a free land, and now they're gonna take it from us. Why must they always chase after the Jews? Why? Why? Why?

LOUIS   It says here how much they're gonna pay for it.

JANKOV   Kids, start packin'! I always hated this place. It's a slum. Poisons everywhere.

REBEKAH falls into the river, starts splashing about and calling for help. JULIA runs to her, helps her up.

LOUIS   Whaddaya say we get a bungalow?

JANKOV   I'd like a pool.

LOUIS   Heart-shaped or kidney?

LOUIS &
JANKOV   Why not both?

REBEKAH becomes ELIZABETH LeBreton.

ELIZABETH   And that brings us to "A Petition Read by An Aged Indian Seeking the Restitution of His Land."

Train whistle.

But it's time to go, I'm afraid. Will you see us to the train station?

BILL	All aboard! I've always wanted to say that. Here we go.
LOUISE	Bye, mom.
JULIA	Have you got everything?
LOUISE	Of course, we only checked like twenty gazillion times.
JULIA	Okay.
BILL	Bye, hon.
JULIA	Bye. And don't forget to–
BILL	We're not calling.
JULIA	Just to let me know you got there.
BILL	No! Louise, let's go.
JULIA	Wait. *(she hugs LOUISE)*
ELIZABETH	Well, Miss Wright. Here's our train. Thank you for your kindness towards uncle. If there's anything we can do for you.
JULIA	There is.
	Train whistle.
LOUISE	Hi mummy.
JULIA	Hello. Where's your father?
LOUISE	Getting the bags. Oh mummy I missed you so much.
JULIA	Did you have a good time?
LOUISE	Yes, and we've decided to do it every year. Only *you* have to promise to come with us.

JULIA	Deal.

Train whistle.

ELIZABETH	And now we really must go.
JULIA	Yes, but – your uncle – he asked me to check in on you now and again.
ELIZABETH	Whatever for?
JULIA	Just to make sure you're alright.
ELIZABETH	How perfectly ridiculous. You couldn't even look after your own.

BILL appears.

BILL	Don't do this to yourself.
JULIA	I never got to hold her.
BILL	Julia–
JULIA	I should have been there.
BILL	Listen to me.
JULIA	I should never have let you go.
BILL	I went back. I did. I just, I needed to go. I didn't plan it, I just, I needed to go there, and I went. I stood there, stood there on the spot we'd been, yes, and I could feel her there. I walked to the river, it was so powerful, it just hit me. I could feel her. I want you to–
JULIA	No.
BILL	Listen, I want you to go.
JULIA	I can't.

BILL	To go, to feel what – you can't do this, you can't hold onto her like this for the rest of your–
JULIA	Get out getoutgetout!

THE PARTY

STAN's house.

STAN	Julia?
JULIA	Hello, Stan.
STAN	Well – wonderful! I – you missed the food, but–
JULIA	It's alright.
STAN	Come in, come. Can I get you a drink? Look everyone, Julia's here.
DAVIDSON	Julia! Hey!
DANIELLE	Hi!
JULIA	Hello, hello.
ROBYN	Hello, Miss Wright.
DAVIDSON	We're having a time. Stan was just about to show us his architectural drawings.
DANIELLE	Shut up, Davidson.
DAVIDSON	Come on, Stan, bring 'em on.
STAN	No, no.
DAVIDSON	Yes, yes. Stan! Stan!
DANIELLE	*(joining in)* Stan! Stan!

ROBYN, DANIELLE & DAVIDSON	Stan! Stan! Stan!
STAN	Alright, al*right*! Julia, come on in now. (*holding his portfolio case*) Now, look, these are from a long time ago, so–
DAVIDSON	Enough with the excuses, bring 'em on.

STAN shows them.

STAN	I haven't even looked at them myself for some time. Just gathering dust in the study.

They look at the drawings.

DANIELLE	Stan–
ROBYN	Wow–
DAVIDSON	Stan, these are – you did these?
STAN	Now, I know you're joking, Davidson, so–
DAVIDSON	I'm not joking. I'm absolutely stunned.
STAN	Are you?
DANIELLE	Look at this one.
STAN	Yes, my tower. Well, it was part of an exercise, based on the idea of the Garden City. Le Corbusier, you know. The wealthy would live in luxury homes; everyone else would be in skyscrapers. Municipal buildings to the left and right. Surrounded by museums and the universities. The city was to be a great park. Anyway, we were to design one element of it. I chose a skyscraper. It's somewhat ornate, I can see that now.

DAVIDSON	Not at all, not at all. This is exactly the kind of building we need in this city.
STAN	You see how the glass would have allowed for the play of shadow and light. The idea was that it should work with its surroundings.
DANIELLE	Stan, why didn't you go on with this?
STAN	Well... it's... well, that's enough of that.

> *The others protest, "no, no, show us some more." He starts to gather up the drawings.*

	I don't want to monopolize the evening. Besides, it's time – for the fortune cookies. *(handing them out)* Here we go, Danielle, there's one for you – Davidson – Robyn.
DAVIDSON	Some crazy party.
STAN	Julia.
JULIA	No thank you.
STAN	Oh yes. Everyone gets one. Come on, let's crack them open.
DAVIDSON	*(opens his)* Now this one is unusual.
STAN	What does it say?
DAVIDSON	"How do you keep an Indian occupied? See other side." *(flips it over)* "How do you keep an Indian occupied...
DANIELLE	Ohhh–
ROBYN	Boo–
DAVIDSON	...see other side."

STAN	That's really terrible.
DAVIDSON	That's what it says!
STAN	Oh look. Mine's interesting. It says, "Help, I'm being held prisoner in a cookie factory," ha ha ha ha!
DAVIDSON	Stan, that is the oldest goddamn joke in–
DANIELLE	Oh yours was *much* better, Davidson.
STAN	Julia, you haven't opened yours.
DANIELLE	Well, I'll go then. *(reading hers)* "Follow your heart and you will be happy."

The others say "awwwwww."

I'm keeping this.

DAVIDSON	Yeah, tape it to your fridge.
DANIELLE	I will.
DAVIDSON	Cause that's meant *only* for you.
DANIELLE	What if it is?
STAN	Robyn, how about you?
ROBYN	'Kay. *(She tries to open hers.)* "Follow your heart and"–
DAVIDSON	*(laughing and pointing at DANIELLE)* Ha ha ha!
DANIELLE	Ferme la trap, Davidson.
DAVIDSON	That's the funniest thing I've ever – a ha ha ha ha ha!
DANIELLE	Yeah. *(She balls hers up and throws it away.)* Fucking hilarious.

DAVIDSON	Well, that was a scream. What next? Jacks? Charades?
STAN	Now hold on. Julia hasn't read hers.
JULIA	I'd rather not.
ROBYN	Why?
JULIA	I just–
DAVIDSON	It's just a freakin' cookie.
	He takes it.
STAN	No funny business now.
DAVIDSON	Yeah yeah.
	He opens it; there's nothing inside.
STAN	Well, isn't that the damndest thing?
DANIELLE	Davidson, you hid it.
DAVIDSON	I did *not*.
STAN	Son of a gun. I've never seen that before. I think I'm gonna call the restaurant.
JULIA	Look–
STAN	No, this just isn't right. I mean, there are certain things that just aren't right and–
JULIA	Stan, forget it, alright? I didn't want one anyway. I need to use your phone. *(beat)* Is there something wrong with my wanting to use the phone?
STAN	Of course not.
JULIA	Could you tell me where it is, then?

STAN	There's one in the study. I'll show you.
JULIA	Just – tell me where it is.
STAN	Out this door, turn left, first room on the right.

JULIA goes to the study. Makes a phone call.

JULIA	*(listens)* Tom, hi... it's me... Saturday night, around ten... um... it's Julia by the way... I'm at this party. But I have no idea why... I came looking for a sign, and I'm afraid I got one.... Anyway, I was hoping to drop by later tonight.... It's about your survey lessons, you see. I was thinking about your last assignment, and I'm afraid you didn't go nearly far enough with your explorations, so... I'm afraid I'm going to have to keep you after class for some private tutorials...

STAN enters.

...well, I guess you're out scouting or... I need to talk to you, to see you, to be with you, I have no idea why, I just...

She turns, sees STAN.

...so if you could make sure the cats have plenty of fresh water, that would be terrific. Thanks.

She hangs up. Pause.

STAN	You seemed upset. I thought perhaps I might have–
JULIA	No. Suddenly realized I hadn't been home for a while and – the cats, they–

STAN	Of course. Well. *(beat; nods towards the window)* Nice view, isn't it?
JULIA	Lovely.
STAN	We had the windows put in to expand it. The view. The trees are spectacular in the fall.
JULIA	I'm sure they are.
STAN	Yes. Do you know, I was sitting in here one day. I like to read here, it's a lovely spot for it, very calm, you know. Well, on this one day, I was having trouble concentrating on the book. I kept looking up, staring out the window. And then I noticed my reflection, faintly, just the outlines of my body. Well as the sun began to set, as light disappeared outside, I noticed that my reflection was growing stronger, more vivid. The details started to get filled in, and pretty soon, when it was pitch black outside and bright as day inside, I could see myself, fully reflected. And I thought, yes, well it's only when things are darkest, you know, that we see ourselves most clearly. *(beat)* I wish you'd have told me.
JULIA	Told you.
STAN	That you have a – that you're with someone. I mean. I've said so many things. Things which. Well. I feel like something of a fool at the moment.
JULIA	You're not a fool.
STAN	And you came to the house. I took it as a sign, I suppose. It's not surprising, I guess, that I got it wrong. I should have learned a long time ago that nothing turns out. No.
JULIA	Why don't we go back?

STAN	I've seen us here. Out there. Walking along the path. Maybe I shouldn't tell you these things. Should I?

She shakes her head no.

I'm in love with you. You're in my mind, all the time, Julia, all the time. You said the other day, what was it, that we can never be happy, wasn't that it, that we could only remember being happy? Well, I don't accept that. Terrible things have happened to us. We could comfort each other.

JULIA	I lost my child.
STAN	I can help you.
JULIA	You can't, though. Please don't say any more, would you?
STAN	Julia, please, I'm in love with you. I see us together. I see us here, in these rooms, and out there, and we *are* happy, do you understand? We *have* children.
JULIA	Stop it. You can't say these things.
STAN	Is it so wrong? Is it? To want to start over? We're young. We – we have so much to–
JULIA	Stan. We have no future. Do you understand?

They hear the others, who enter after a moment.

STAN	Yes, yes, and some of those trees are as old as – oh, hello folks, we were just chatting about the trees and all that.
DAVIDSON	Trees. Good. Listen to this, though. Go ahead, kid, tell her.

ROBYN	Well, it's an idea I got yesterday, when we were talking about finding someone who used to live on the Flats, I got the idea to *do* that.
DAVIDSON	Don't you love this kid?
ROBYN	I got a list of people and everything, and I started going through the phone book, and I found one! Her name's Dolores Couillard. Her family used to *own* the Duke House, like in the 30s and stuff. I told her what we were doing, and said could I talk to her, and she's like, yeah whatever. So I went to see her this afternoon, it was totally amazing. She had this huge photo album— she called it her "memory book"—and she showed me just everything. It was so weird, I felt like I was really walking down the street with her. It was just really magical. And her stories! The changes she's seen in her lifetime. She was this really cool lady. And then on the last page, there was a shot of the Duke House, just standing alone. You could see the wrecking ball in the background. Dolores, she told me that everyone who lived on the Flats went to the Duke that night, the night of the photo. It was St Patrick's Day, and everyone came to say goodbye. They sang Irish songs— "even the French," she said—they drank, they cried, and the next day they gathered at the top of the cliff, and watched it being torn down. Gone. And there's nothing, you know, not a plaque, not a marker, not anything, to say what was there. Or who.
STAN	Why should there be? Why should they be remembered? They were there, that's all.
	Pause.
ROBYN	I asked her, I hope you don't mind, Miss Wright, if she would come and talk to us. She's never been back. Is it alright?

DANIELLE	Just as long as Davidson doesn't tell her what he's planning down there.
DAVIDSON	Hey.
DANIELLE	She might not like too much what's gonna cut across her old home, uh?
JULIA	What's that?
DANIELLE	Davidson was showing us his designs for the Flats.
DAVIDSON	Very early sketches.
JULIA	Do you mean just now? You were showing the designs just now?
DAVIDSON	"Designs" is a little grandiose. It's just some doodles. You wanna see 'em?
JULIA	Very much, yes.
	DAVIDSON pulls a sheet out of his pocket.
DANIELLE	Professional as always.
DAVIDSON	Like I said, it's a doodle. I've superimposed some ideas onto this aerial photo. Now here's the Flats. This is the area which–
STAN	Do you know – sorry – I've never realized before. I always thought it was a square. But looking at it now, it actually looks like a circle.
DAVIDSON	Yeah that's good, Stan. Next we'll see if you can spell your name with blocks. Now–
STAN	*Stop it! (beat)* I mean, there's just so much one can take, Davidson. Finally, there's just so much.

DAVIDSON	Okay, Stan.
STAN	Well. Go on, then.
DAVIDSON	Now, Duke Street is going to form one side of the Great Park. A huge open space, with great views of the water and Parliament Hill. People will come out here, play, jog, have picnics, whatever, but they'll *use* this place, it'll be a centre of life, and in constant use. Now who here has read Jane Jacobs? Anyone? Well, Jane Jacobs is what I call an urban thinker, not a planner exactly, she never had any training, she was just someone who *saw things*, and wrote about them, in a tough and fearless way. See, she's all about multi-use, about high density, about street life, constant activity. That's why we're gonna have, in addition to high income housing here, here and here – we're gonna have three skyscrapers, boom boom boom. Stan, that's why your tower blew me away, this is exactly what–
JULIA	What's this line here?
DAVIDSON	I'll get to that. You see, Stan–
JULIA	But what's this line here?
DAVIDSON	I said I'll get to it.
JULIA	But what is it?
DAVIDSON	It's the parkway. I had to move it away from the river, to make room for the housing.
JULIA	Put it back.
DAVIDSON	Uh huh. Anyway, Stan, the point is–
JULIA	I said put it back.

DAVIDSON   Tell you what. You do the surveying. I'll
                do the–

JULIA   It's because of my survey that I'm telling
                you: you can't put the parkway there.

DAVIDSON   Why not?

JULIA   Because that's my acre. That's my acre.

DAVIDSON   Hell's she talkin' about?

                JULIA grabs the paper.

                Hey!

JULIA   You can't put a parkway across my acre.

DAVIDSON   Would you give me that back?

JULIA   You want it back?

DAVIDSON   Yes, I want it–

JULIA   Here. *(rips it in half)*

DAVIDSON   Okay.

JULIA   *(keeps ripping) Get* me, I'm making
                subdivisons.

DAVIDSON   Very funny, yeah.

JULIA   Land for sale! Land for sale! Who needs a
                lot? Oh look– *(throws the paper in the air)*
                A land grab. Bulwark! I'll see *you* in court.
                Who wants land? Anyone? Anyone? *(to
                ROBYN)* Ohmigod, isn't this awesome? *(to
                DAVIDSON)* Ah, Davidson, come in. Well,
                I've had a chance to look at your plans and,
                well, they're shit. Get out.

DAVIDSON   Guess some of us hold our booze better
                than others.

JULIA	This ain't the booze talkin', honey.
DAVIDSON	Well, whatever it is, it's a fuckin' idiot.
JULIA	Is that right? Why? Because it doesn't like your plans? Hm? Well, I guess it oughta shut up, then, eh Davidson? It oughta shut up and praise your plans. There. It's quiet now. Shh. Listen. Do you hear it? *Progress!* *Look out, coming through!* Hey, Davidson, get outta my way, get outta my way Davidson, coming through–
DAVIDSON	Are you out of your mind?
JULIA	Progress, can't stop progress.
DAVIDSON	No, you can't. Much as you'd like to. I suppose you'd rather see the Flats stay empty. Well, guess what? People need to live somewhere, know what I mean? Unless you'd rather see more sprawl. Is that what you want?
JULIA	Not me, boy.
DAVIDSON	No, good. Now if you've got a better idea of how to plan this space, you go ahead and tell me. It's easy to tear up another guy's ideas, but if you do, you'd better have some of your own. Go ahead, I'm all ears.
JULIA	But I have no ideas.
DAVIDSON	Didn't think so.
JULIA	Still, can I tell you why your plan's never going to work?
DAVIDSON	Spare me.
JULIA	You can't create happiness, Davidson, that's why. Your picnics in the park are a crock.

You're a pitch man, selling memories-in-a-bottle. But if I may be allowed to shatter your glassy illusions, no one's going to use that park because you show them that they *can*; they'll use it because it feels right and natural to do so, and that's not something you can predict.

DAVIDSON   Well that's where–

JULIA   You want people to imagine some lovely future, don't you, Davidson? A future that holds no regard for the past. History is bunk, said the car maker; history is dead, says the planner. But it's the past that's in front of us – we can see it. It comes towards us, it won't be forgotten. And if you try to bury it, you might as well bury yourself with it. You know, there's one little thing you neglected to mention as you extolled the virtues of Jane Jacobs and her fearless vision, one essential element you seem not to have noticed.

DAVIDSON   And what's that?

JULIA   Time. Time, Davidson. And that's not something you can put into a plan. It's not something you can get your hands on. But it's essential. A place needs time to become what it's going to be. A place, a child. *(beat)* You, Davidson, you think you can cheat time, you think you can steal its power, like some modern Prometheus. Well none of us can do that. None of us have found a way. But, who knows, young genius, maybe you'll find a way to do it. And if you do, I hope I come back as the great bird that pecks away at your liver for all eternity.

(She scoops up the paper.) Here you are. Congratulations. The future's in the palm of your hand.

She goes.

JULIA   (*to the commission*) I ran back to the Flats. I needed to be with Tom. But when I got there, the trailer was gone. There was no sign of him at all.

I found my branch, raised it high above my head and brought it down hard, again and again and again, over yellow sweet clover, wild indigo, chicory, daisies, again and again and–

DOLORES

DOLORES Couillard stands there.

DOLORES   *Fais attention*! *Fais attention*! Watch it with that stick!

JULIA   Sorry, didn't see you there.

DOLORES   What you doing with that stick, anyway?

Pause.

JULIA   Survey.

DOLORES   Survey? Nothing here to survey. Used to be. Was beautiful community, uh?

Pause.

Homes here. Stores. All up and down this street, people. Right here, my home. Duke House. Everybody look out for me. "*Fais attention*," they say, when I go play in the street, "*fais attention*, Dolores. *Fais attention*."

JULIA   Dolores – Couillard?

DOLORES   That's me.

JULIA

Born here?

DOLORES

Sure. In the middle of an earthquake. Look at that – I'm still shaking. *(She bursts out laughing.)*

JULIA

You never came back?

DOLORES

Come back? Nothing here. What was real – gone. Only thing now – poison. Up there? By the river? Junk yard. Old cars, they bring in, take apart. The oils, they dump into the ground. Poison. Over there – paint factory. Poison. The city, they use this place to dump snow, uh? Mountains of snow, and when it melts, poisons, from the street, into the ground. Poison.

Pause.

I don't need to come here. You know where it is, all what was here? In my mind. When I want to remember, I go in there. Nobody tear it down.

Pause.

When I die, this gonna be my heaven. When I was a girl, I go to church, the preacher he say "be good, or you gonna burn!" My friends, they were so scared. Big eyes, like this. Not me. I think, the place we gonna go, we make it ourselves. The last thing we think about, that gonna be where we spend all time. So I'm gonna think about this place. What you gonna think about Julia, when you old like me?

LOUISE

Mother! Mother help me!

DOLORES

That what you want?

LOUISE, gasping for breath.

	No, Julia. Nothing you could do. You know that. Have to get rid of it, Julia. Get rid of this poison. You know why you come here. *(Pause.)* What you want, Julia?
JULIA	Time. Time with her. "Give yourself time," they said. But it isn't mine to give. It's only something that can be taken, and it was, taken from me, time with her, and I ache, I ache, from every muscle, every fibre, every part of me, I ache for time with my girl.
DOLORES	She had her time, Julia. You had it with her.
LOUISE	*(appearing)* Oh, mummy, look!
DOLORES	Get rid of the poison.
LOUISE	Chicory.
DOLORES	Poison inside you.
LOUISE	And clover.
DOLORES	Get rid of it.
LOUISE	And here! White daisies!
DOLORES	And when it's gone–
LOUISE	He loves me, he loves me not–
DOLORES	You think only of this.
LOUISE	Oh no my bracelet!
DOLORES	And you go to heaven.
LOUISE	Mummy, will you help me?
DOLORES	You be there with her, for all time. This what you want, Julia?
JULIA	Oh yes.

DOLORES   Then go. Be with her.

LOUISE   Will you help me?

DOLORES   *Fais attention. Fais attention*, Julia.

    She goes.

BILL   Kiddo, we'll look for it after lunch.

LOUISE   Oh!

BILL   C'mon, let's eat, I'm starving. What have we got here? Chicken. Brraaaaak! Say, listen, what do you think would happen if we all had to kill our dinner?

LOUISE   Gross!

BILL   No, I mean it.

JULIA   Do we *have* to discuss this now.

BILL   Just listen. If we actually had to *hunt* – I mean the way people *did*. We'd all be vegetarians.

LOUISE   Not if we had respect for the animals. If we thanked them for what they gave us.

BILL   You mean like this? *(to the sandwich)* Hey, thanks. *(bites into it)*

LOUISE   No! We don't have any respect for the land.

BILL   Is that a fact?

LOUISE   I read it in a book. "Ancient Rituals of the First Peoples." It says the natives used to have rituals for everything. Like, when they'd kill an animal, they'd eat a piece of its liver or something the moment its spirit left.

JULIA	Puh-leez.
LOUISE	They would!
JULIA	Not during lunch!
LOUISE	They would! That way, you'd make sure of having another successful hunt.
BILL	And how exactly did they know when the spirit left?
LOUISE	They just did.
BILL	What else is in that book?
LOUISE	Well, a family's territory, the nokiwaki, would–
BILL	Nooky wooky.
LOUISE	No! The territory wasn't marked out with fences or anything, it was just understood.
BILL	Geez, honey, you'd be out of a job.
JULIA	Wouldn't I just.
BILL	Sounds like the Indians didn't go for straight lines.
LOUISE	No. Circles. They believed in eternity. There was no end to life. That's why you always had to leave enough for the next generation. Like, you should never take more than two-thirds of the adult beavers in one hunting season.
BILL	Just like my college days.
JULIA	Don't bother.
LOUISE	And my total favourite? A white animal coming into the territory was considered bad luck.

BILL	Yeah, well, it was bad luck when the white man came along, that's fer durn sure.
LOUISE	But they knew that, Daddy.
BILL	Knew what, sweetheart.
LOUISE	Knew that when the whites came, it meant their own way of life would be destroyed. They knew they were going to die.
JULIA	Alright, can we just leave the Indians behind for now? I am just enjoying this day.
BILL	*(sings)* "I would swim over the deepest ocean/The deepest ocean to be by your side."
	BILL and LOUISE giggle.
JULIA	Alright, what's going on here?
BILL	*(to LOUISE)* Do you want to tell her, or–?
JULIA	Tell me–?
LOUISE	We're going to go away! Just me and Daddy, next weekend, up north!
JULIA	What?
LOUISE	We're going to take the train, and rent a cottage, and go sailing, oh mother, please, please, please–
JULIA	Whoa, whoa, *whoa*. Whose idea was *this?*
BILL	Uh – yours.
JULIA	Mine?
BILL	Well, I've been away a lot this year, you said the two of us should spend more time together, so I – I thought it'd be nice if – forget it.

LOUISE	Oh!
BILL	No, no. Your mother's tacit disapproval has reared its–
JULIA	You could at least have–
BILL	You can't control her every move.
LOUISE	Please don't fight. Please! We're having such a lovely day. Mother. It's just for the weekend. It'll be so much fun. Please let me go. Please let me go!
BILL	I need time with her, too, Julia. You said so yourself.

Pause.

LOUISE	Look.

BILL does a bird whistle.

It's a partridge.

BILL	See that? It's a sign. She's gotta leave the nest sometime.
JULIA	What?
BILL	I mean come on. She's never been away from home. Not for a single night. Know what I mean?

Pause.

JULIA	You're not going.
LOUISE	Oh!
BILL	What?
JULIA	It's white. "When a white animal–"

BILL	Oh come on! You're not serious!
LOUISE	Mother, it's just a silly old superstition. Please. You have to let me go. Let me go.
	JULIA takes LOUISE by the hand. Kisses her. Releases her.
	After a moment, BILL begins to reprise the song: "But the sea is wide, and I can't swim over—"

THE DUKE HOUSE

	And the scene shifts into the Duke House where all have gathered to say goodbye.
ALL BUT JULIA	—and neither have I wings to fly / I wish I could find me a handy boatman to ferry me over to my love and die.
	The others continue to hum the tune throughout.
IRISHMAN	Ah, it's a grand day for a wake. Here we are, gathered together at the Duke House, the last building left on the Flats. Who'd like to say a few words? Don't be shy.
LEBRETON	Right, as the man who gave his name to this property, I fink it's only fitting that I should be the one to pay its last respects.
DALHOUSIE	Still clinging to your unethical grip on the land, LeBreton?
LEBRETON	—wot?
DOLORES	You speak, Julia.
JULIA	I can't.

ALL BUT JULIA	My childhood days bring back sad reflections, of happy times spent so long ago.
CHAMPLAIN	Very well, then, I shall speak. After all, it was I, Samuel de Champlain, who discovered this land, and claimed it in the name of Louis the– *(counts on his fingers)*
SOPHIA	15th! I learnt that in school, I did.
CHAMPLAIN	Charming child. How old are you?

> *SOPHIA punches CHAMPLAIN in the stomach.*

LEBRETON	Serves you right, Croaker!
ALL BUT JULIA	My childhood friends and my own relations have all passed on now like the melting snow.

> *Crash from the wrecking ball.*

DOLORES	Hurry, Julia, say something!
JULIA	I can't!
ALL BUT JULIA	But I'll spend my days in endless roving, soft sit the grass my bed is free.

> *Crash. They continue to hum.*

STEGMANN	Ya, okay, I speak now. You know, it's funny but, so when I first come here, I noted that all around was a tedious swamp and all this, and I wrote that this place was unfit for culture. And now, of course, almost two hundred years later – it seems I was right.

> *Crash.*

ALL BUT JULIA	Oh to be home now in Carrickfergus / On the long road down to the salty sea.

ELIZABETH	Miss Wright, it's time for you to offer a few words of condolence.
THE OTHERS	Speech! Speech!
ELIZABETH	No one else can do it, Miss Wright. We're gone.
	Crash.
JULIA	I don't know what to say.
	Crash.
	I don't know what to say!
IRISHMAN	What happened to the singin'?
ALL BUT JULIA	I'm drunk today, and I'm seldom sober, a handsome rover from town to town–
	TOM appears. The others continue to hum.
JULIA	Are you here?
TOM	Nope. Halifax. Full day shooting tomorrow. *(looking around)* The gang's all here.
JULIA	Not quite. Constant Penency. I can't hear him. Can't see him.
TOM	Not his crowd. He's waiting for them to clear out. You get my note?
JULIA	Where?
TOM	Your pocket.
	He goes. She gets the note.
JULIA	"You'll know when I return."
ALL	I'm drunk today, and I'm rarely sober–

IRISHMAN	Come on, Julia, you too!
ALL	Ah, but I am sick now, and my days are numbered–
	The others fade away. JULIA is alone.
JULIA	–so come all ye young ones, and lay me down.
	ROBYN stands there.
ROBYN	Hello, Miss Wright.
	Pause.
JULIA	Excuse me. (*picks up the branch*) The third corner. Did you know there used to be a tavern here?
ROBYN	The Duke House.
JULIA	Right. Forgot. You know everything. (*lays down the branch*) One.
ROBYN	Why don't you like me?
JULIA	Who says?
ROBYN	You. The way you are with me. From the beginning. I mean, all I wanted to do was be helpful. That's all.
JULIA	Oh you've been that alright.
ROBYN	There, you see? You're always so sarcastic with me. (*beat*) Why won't you talk to me?
	Pause.
JULIA	Two.
ROBYN	What are you doing?

JULIA

Measuring out my acre, what's it look like. Two more turns of the branch and I'll be back where I started.

ROBYN

Look, Julia. I mean, is it alright if I call you that?

JULIA

You just did.

ROBYN

Danielle told me about your daughter. (*Pause.*) I was asking her, you see. I wanted to know why you didn't like me. She said—Danielle said—probably because I remind you of her. I said, I don't understand. Then why *wouldn't* you like me?

JULIA

(*looking at her*) Because you're everything she never got to be. Because you're bright and lovely, and you have your future. Because when I saw you for the first time, you took my breath away. Because every time you speak, you remind me of what's been taken away from me. And no, it isn't right, and no, it isn't fair, but it is, it just is, and I wish, I wish everyone would stop, just stop stop stop trying to tell me to get over it, or what to do, or how to be. Three.

She brings down the branch.

ROBYN

I'm not, though. I would never do that. I'm going away tomorrow. Sailing to Europe. I'm spending the rest of the summer there. I wanted you to have something. (*hands JULIA the bracelet*) I found it here. I thought to keep it to myself, but, after Danielle told me everything, I thought I should give it to you instead.

JULIA takes a quick look at it, looks away.

JULIA

Just put it down there, would you?

ROBYN   Alright. *(She does.)* I'd like to call you when
                   I get back.

                   JULIA nods.

                   I'm going now.

                   ROBYN goes.

JULIA   *(to the commission)* I picked up the bracelet.
                   The one my daughter had lost that day on
                   the Flats. I slipped it onto my wrist. As I
                   sat there, heat returned. I was hoping the
                   partridge would come back, too, but there
                   was no sign of him. Not yet, not yet. I lay
                   down the branch one last time. My survey
                   was complete. And I understood then why
                   I had been sent to this place.

                   I was asked to survey an empty field. I am
                   asking that one acre of this field remain
                   empty, for all time. Build your offices,
                   your homes, your parkway, build what you
                   like, but leave this one acre as a place of
                   remembrance, where the living may come
                   to honour the dead. To calm the spirits
                   here, the angry as well as the playful, the
                   loving as well as the lost.

                   Yes, I wrote of rituals. Of respect. Of
                   rebirth.

                   And as I sat on the earth, in that place
                   where she and I had been, I understood: it
                   was I who was to be reborn. That the future
                   I had imagined for my daughter would
                   perhaps one day be mine. And she would
                   lead me to it.

                   I slipped off the bracelet, and placed it on
                   the fourth corner, Goodbye, my darling.
                   Lay still this day.

                   The end.